Building
in
Love

Building in Love

The Vocation of the Church

Editors:
John Greenhalgh, Elizabeth Russell

St Mary's Bourne Street

First published 1990
St Mary's, Bourne Street
St Mary's Presbytery
30 Bourne Street
London SW1W 8JJ

ISBN 0 9508516 4 7

British Library Cataloguing in Publication Data

Building in Love: the Vocation of the Church.
1. Christian Church. Mission
I. Russell, Elizabeth, *1921–*   II. Greenhalgh, John 266

ISBN 0 9508516 4 7

Photoset in Souvenir and Times by Input Typesetting Ltd, London
Printed in Great Britain by Billing & Sons Ltd, Book Plan, Hylton Road,
Worcester

Contents

Preface

The editors

THIS is the fifth volume in the series **Tracts for Our Times**, the first of which marked the 150th anniversary of the beginning of the Oxford Movement. The two volumes which immediately preceded *Building in Love – 'If Christ be not risen . . .'* and *Signs of Faith, Hope and Love* – dealt with theological themes: the resurrection and the sacraments, and how we perceive them today.

In *Building in Love* there is a change of direction. Bearing in mind that 1990 marks another beginning, that of a decade of evangelism, we have tried to tease out some aspects of the vocation of the Christian Church at the end of the twentieth century in Britain.

Some very important issues are omitted or barely mentioned. There is, for example, very little on the crucial duty of the Church in politics or social action, and even less on the question of women priests. These gaps are not accidental. A wide range of published material on these subjects is readily available.

Moreover, the object of this book is not to be controversial so much as to give our contributors the opportunity to write on subjects which, although they are bound to be affected by the present situation, are essentially part of the permanent vocation of the Church: teaching the Faith, caring for the flock, bringing the world into the light of the word. This vocation is a serious topic and one on which all Christians feel deeply.

It is probably a good idea not to try to read these essays all at one sitting, rather to dip into the book article by article; otherwise, the reader may find the content settling a little heavily on the mind's stomach and producing a sense of moral indigestion. We trust, however, that, as a whole, the book will give some indication of the richness and variety of thought of British Christians on the mission of the Church in our time, and that you will find it of personal use.

The contributors are drawn, as they say, 'from all walks of life' and are, in the main, very busy people. We would like to thank them for agreeing to take part, free, gratis and for nothing, in writing this book. In our choice of contributors we have turned for advice to John Gilling, Nicholas Kavanagh and Martin Dudley, whose assistance has been indispensable, and our thanks are once again due also to SCM Press for its work in pre-publication publicity and distribution.

John Greenhalgh is the verger of St Mary's Bourne Street and Elizabeth Russell a member of the congregation. Both have publishing experience.

Apprehending joy: the imagination

Brian Horne

IN THE LIBRARY of the presbytery of St Mary's Church, Bourne Street, London there hangs a portrait of one of the most distinguished churchmen of the modern era: John Henry, Cardinal Newman. It is a picture that would probably confirm the impression which many people have had of this notable priest and scholar: austere, ascetic, cold, inflexible and, above all, intellectual. Newman was, perhaps, all of these things from time to time, but he was also very much more, and he was far from being representative of those who believe in the power of the human mind to penetrate the mysteries of God. This was a man who spent much of his time and energy in the writing of poetry; whose long dramatic poem *The Dream of Gerontius* inspired one of Edward Elgar's most intense and romantic works; who gave English men and women one of their favourite hymns: that passionate and personal expression of frailty and faith, "Lead, kindly Light". This was a man who saw as clearly as any of his contemporaries, and as clearly as any theologian and preacher, that being a Christian involved far more than obedience to the Church or conscience; more than intellectual conviction and emotional commitment. Important as these might be, and necessary as they were, the essence of faith went beyond them and was more mysterious than any of them.

Towards the end of his life he tried to describe and analyse this mysterious heart of religion in a book to which he gave the title *An Essay in aid of a Grammar of Assent*. It is a book which addresses, among other things, the problem of the relationship between faith and reason, and asks the question "why and how do we believe?";

9

in other words, "what is happening when we believe?" In answering it he draws a most important distinction; a distinction between two kinds of "assent": "notional" assent and "real" assent. By notional assent is meant the kind of assent that is given to something – a concept or a proposition – that is known to be true but does not materially affect the lives of those who give it. We make this kind of assent all the time to all kinds of things without our lives being changed by the act. No consequences for our behaviour or our attitudes, our desires or hopes follow from this act of notional assent. But, there is another kind of assent and one which has the most far-reaching consequences in our lives; an assent which, when it is given, shapes and directs our whole personality, which gives us new hopes and different desires. For this kind of assent, which was at the heart of Christian faith, Newman chose the word "real"; or, at least, he proposed the word "real" for the text of the book which was eventually published in 1870. But the manuscripts in which he prepared the book tell a different story. Newman had another word in mind for describing this kind of conviction and that word was "imaginative".[1] His original intention was to point the contrast between an assent that was little more than an intellectual acknowledgement of a truth i.e. something "notional", and an assent that engaged the whole personality of the believer in that which was acknowledged i.e. something "imaginative". Far from being a cold and inflexible rationalist he was a man who had discerned the central and decisive part played by the imagination in the development of the human personality and, most particularly, in the human creature's response to its Creator. It is not, perhaps, surprising that Newman abandoned his original intention; the word was too shocking. Even today, "imagination" sounds strange in the context of theological discussion; it is associated with the concept of art rather than with that of religion and so with the artist rather than that of the believer – and so artistic and religious responses are driven apart. Perhaps Newman felt that the concept was liable to be misconstrued and, in the disputatious world of academic theology, even ridiculed. But, he never abandoned the insight he had gained and throughout the long essay *The Grammar of Assent* we feel the pressure of his belief in the power of the imagination; we see him trying to discover and articulate the means by which the human being lays hold upon and makes real Christian truth; we see him exploring and explaining a process that is best defined as a process of the imagination.

The idea that one should grasp the truths of the Christian religion and respond to them by imagination is an idea that would have startled thinkers before the eighteenth century. This is partly explained by the history of the word itself. In the last act of *A Midsummer Night's Dream* Shakespeare gives a speech to Theseus on the subject of the imagination.

> . . . . I never may believe
> These antique fables, nor these fairy toys.
> Lovers and madmen have such seething brains,
> Such shaping fantasies, that apprehend
> More than cool reason ever comprehends.
> The lunatic, the lover, and the poet
> Are of imagination all compact:
>
> And, as imagination bodies forth
> The forms of things unknown, the poet's pen
> Turns them to shapes, and gives to airy nothing
> A local habitation and a name.
> Such tricks hath strong imagination
> That, if it would but apprehend some joy,
> It comprehends some bringer of that joy;
> Or, in the night, imagining some fear,
> How easy is a bush supposed a bear![2]

Until two centuries ago the word was usually used to describe the mental capacity to fantasise and fabricate dreams; a realm inaccessible to Reason; a power which could sever the connection between the mind and the real world of fact and sensation; illusory, phantasmagoric. It was powerful and dangerous and was, on that account, feared and rejected by philosophers and theologians. It still had some of these connotations in Newman's day and it retains them in our own. But, what Newman was talking about was not imagination in this sense. As a child of the Romantic movement he had inherited from the thinkers and poets of the early part of the nineteenth century a richer, more complex notion of the imagination.[3] Furthermore, he was convinced that although he was using a new word, or rather, an old word in a new sense, he was describing and analysing a phenomenon that was not at all new, but was as old as mankind itself: a process which was a vital part of the way in which the human being recognised the truth both about himself and about God.

What then is "imagination"? And why is it crucial both to our understanding of ourselves and our apprehension of God? Owen Barfield approaches these questions by way of examining the relationship between matter and spirit. Taking as a basis for his argument the proposition that human beings are a unique compound of the material and the immaterial (in a way that neither angels nor animals are), he asks how the two elements of this compound can be related, and he answers his question with the concept of the imagination.

> It is a fact of immediate experience that, besides being the contradictory of spirit, besides being for that reason the occasion of spirit, and besides being the finished product of spirit (if we so hold), matter can be the present *expression* of spirit. The material can become an image, or picture, of the immaterial. Whether or not it does so for us will depend on ourselves. *When* it does so, we may call the resulting experience "imagination". Imagination, then, also is by its very nature a relation between matter and spirit; but it is a special kind of relation, a relation which at once maintains and transcends that contradiction between the two. . . . Mere perception – perception without imagination – is the sword thrust between spirit and matter.[4]

It is by the power of the imagination that the immaterial is grasped and embodied in the material; that spirit informs matter. It is from this power to unify apparently separate worlds that art becomes possible; for art – music, painting, sculpture, dance – is, in the first instance, matter expressing spirit; the material becoming an image of the immaterial. And the means by which that image is perceived and understood and responded to is, similarly, the imagination. In responding to a poem or a painting we are not simply activating the intellect or opening ourselves to an emotion (though both intellect and emotion are involved), but by a combination of thought and feeling, reason and sensation, which issues in something other; one might almost say, the "feeling intellect" or the "intelligent emotion", namely the imagination.

Even if we accept this as a true picture of the human being, need we be committed to the view that the imagination inevitably plays a crucial role in all religious experience? One would have thought not if one were to argue from a survey of the religions of the world. There are some that teach and practise precisely the opposite. These are the religions that regard spirit and matter as essentially incompatible and mutually exclusive: in all their teaching and discipline they work towards the radical separation of soul and body. Christianity itself, throughout its long history, has constantly been threatened from within by tendencies in the same direction: teachings which regard the body and the whole material world as evil, and practices which have tried to sever the essential (and unbreakable) connection between matter and spirit. But, in her Creeds and Councils, the Church has steadfastly resisted and condemned these tendencies as heretical (the inclusion of the clause "I believe in the resurrection of the dead" in the Nicene Creed is an example) even if she has failed to proclaim with sufficient vigour and persistence what all artists, and some theologians, have always known, that the body "is a unique good" and inseparable from the soul, "holily created and holily raised from the dead".[5] Without this as a fundamental tenet of faith there could be no art and no sacraments. If the body were evil and matter radically incompatible with spirit, gesture and words, stone and wood, paint and sound, would be incapable of embodying and conveying the vision of the artist. If the body were evil and matter essentially antagonistic to spirit, there could be no possibility of bread and wine, water and oil, being the channels, or even the signs, of divine power and grace.

Christianity, above all the religions of the world, should understand and embrace the imagination because of its unique and central teaching: the doctrine of the incarnation. It is a doctrine which celebrates a unique act of imagination: the ultimate manifestation of spirit expressing itself in matter; the archetype which makes all other types of unity between the two worlds possible. Jesus Christ is the very image of God the Father expressed in the material of his own creation. "He is the image of the invisible God, the first-born of all creation" (Colossians 1. 15); "He reflects the glory of God and bears the very stamp of his nature, upholding the universe by the word of his power' (Hebrews 1. 3); "And the Word became flesh and dwelt among us, full of grace and truth" (John 1. 14). Like a sculptor taking clay or wood, God takes the matter of human flesh and enters a material existence to grace it with his own personal power and dignity. The glory of the uncreated God appears in the body of a man, and thus

> In Christ human nature is renewed and saved. The body assumed by God is wholly divinised, transformed . . . crowned with indescribable beauty. It becomes Spirit-bearing. It breaks through the heaviness of earthly matter. Very well; yet on these accounts it does not cease to be truly body.[6]

And how shall this mystery be grasped except by the power of the imagination?

In the story of the transfiguration we are told of the failure of the disciples to understand what was happening when they saw the figure of Jesus radiant with an unearthly splendour. It is not so much a story about lack of faith or the inability of the mind to comprehend the meaning of an event as a story about the failure of the imagination. Only the exercise of that power could have enabled the disciples to discern the reality of the experience and make some kind of coherent response to the vision that they had received. The gospels are full of examples of this kind of failure. Again and again there are instances of the people around Jesus failing to understand the parables or the purpose of the Lord. They have been given all the information they need but while "they may indeed see" they "do not perceive, and may indeed hear but do not understand" (Matthew 4. 12). It is the same with our apprehension of a work of art. The failure to respond is a failure of the imagination. It is not the inability to understand, intellectually, the meaning of the words or the pattern of sounds or colours: one can grasp the "content" of the thing (the "information" supplied by the object) and remain "outside" the work, not discerning the glory. Nor is it a failure to be moved, emotionally, by the thing: the guards of the concentration camps in Nazi Germany were moved to tears by the music of Mozart and Haydn, but could make no connection between their emotions and those of their prisoners whom they herded into the gas ovens. Strong feeling is no sign of the ability to discern the glory. The failure is a failure to bring intellect and emotion together in an act that unites both and transcends both. It is, perhaps, some such perception as this that lies behind the cryptic phrases which end John Keats's poem *Ode on a Grecian Urn*:

> "Beauty is truth, truth beauty," – that is all
> Ye know on earth, and all ye need to know.

The imagination perceives truth and beauty as co-inherent; this is part of what is meant by "discerning the glory".

Will this trivialise Christianity? Is this merely an attempt to turn religion into a kind of aesthetic experience? Does this approach render the Creeds and all attempts at intellectual articulation unnecessary? By no means, but it will put reason and knowledge into their proper perspective and prevent religious fervour from floating aimlessly and self-indulgently. My point is simple: that in examining the way in which we respond to a work of art we find the most important clue to the understanding of what it is that happens when we make a "real" assent to the truths of Christianity as they are revealed in Jesus Christ. The intellect is not abandoned nor do we become cold and unfeeling; and faith is not the conjuring up of pictures that happen to please us. We shall always need to test and understand and be clear about religion at the level of reason; the mind will always need to be fed by the argumentation of theological exposition. And we shall also always need that unthinking emotional drive that will energise work and prayer. But, neither of these is sufficient by itself; they must move into each other in such a way that enables us to respond to God's disclosure of himself in the world. He has created the world after a certain manner: it is a world in which the glory is refracted, is embodied in signs which have to be interpreted, "discerned" in a way that goes beyond what can be supplied by thought and feeling.[7]

In the second act of *Antony and Cleopatra* one of Antony's soldiers speaks of the mysterious beauty of the Egyptian queen.

> Age cannot wither her, nor custom stale
> Her infinite variety; other women cloy
> The appetites they feed; but she makes hungry
> Where most she satisfies.[8]

The effect of this power can be described but its source remains unfathomable. Her beauty cannot be grasped by reason, and feeling is simply the inevitable effect of its being perceived. These few lines can be taken as an expression of an experience that every true believer knows. It is not unlike St Augustine's attempt to articulate his experience of the beauty of God in the tenth book of his *Confessions*:

> I have learnt to love you late, beauty at once so ancient and so new! I have learnt to love you late! You were within me, and I was in the world outside myself. . . . You shone upon me; your radiance enveloped me; you put my blindness to flight. You shed your fragrance about me; I drew breath and now I gasp for your sweet odour. I tasted you, and now I hunger and thirst for joy. You touched me, and I am inflamed with love of your peace.[9]

Again it is imagination that enables St Augustine to discern the glory of God and grasp the meaning of the encounter with God. Faith and humility have been the indispensable preliminaries to this interiorisation of the encounter.

Like a great work of art, the fact of the incarnation – the revelation of God's "person" in the life of Jesus Christ – can be discussed objectively; its theological content can be analysed, but the mysterious source of its power to "enslave" and transform lives can never be plumbed by the theological exposition. And it must be noticed, too, that even the most severely academic theological language, even the terse statements of the Creeds, are fraught with metaphorical suggestion. In the very heart of rational explanation imagination is invoked.[10] The mystery of God (and, for that matter, the mystery of another human being) can only be approached in a way that is analogous to the way in which a work of art is approached: with faith and humility that prepare the ground for imaginative understanding. The first necessity is faith: the trust in the thing itself and its power to enter our lives and change the perceptions we have of ourselves. The second necessity is humility: the freely made decision to allow ourselves to be changed by the experience of that which we are encountering. But, these are only preliminaries to that act of assent which follows. The assent is made as we identify with and enter into the vision of the work of art. This process of identification can only be accomplished by that which I have called the imagination; we are taken out of ourselves as we participate in something that is not ourselves, and so we are returned to ourselves altered by the experience. But, the meaning of the vision does not reveal itself all at once or all in the same way; its power to transform will often only be released over a long period of time and come in ways that cannot be controlled by any act of mind or will or desire of the heart. We should not expect "real" assent to take place instantaneously; it can be the description of a lifetime's surrender.

What is true of the experience of art is supremely true of the experience of God. The response to the work of art is only the shadow, but the true shadow, of the response to the work of God in the incarnation. In faith and humility we approach the fact: the image of God in Christ, the ineffable divinity expressed in the form of a man; by the work of the imagination we are taken out of ourselves and identify with that work of God; in participating in it we are taken into the divine glory which is its centre.

> On the model of the artwork, we should say that it is the splendour of the divine meaning shining in the form of Christ that moves us, transforming our sensibility and habitual vision of things. Only so can we come to "image" that face of God in Jesus by a responding love, ourselves transfigured by grace.[11]

We grasp its meaning and are grasped by it only in so far as our imagination has empowered us to identify ourselves with it; to move out of ourselves into it. The figure of Jesus Christ, like the existence of a work of art, is an objective fact; a particular man in a particular place at a particular moment in the world's history, yet it remains an ultimate mystery: the image of God. It cannot be "explained", it can only be entered into; we cannot make the image, we can only allow the image to make us.

Brian Horne is an honorary assistant priest at St Mary's and a lecturer in Christian doctrine at King's College, London.

Men and women of action

Hugh Beach

What man is he, that feareth the Lord; him shall he teach in the way that he shall choose. (Psalm 25.12)

THE TITLE indicated, "men and women of action" is meant, not as a label of value (still less a price tag of virtue), but as simple description. It points to the world of work rather than to family life or recreation, though these can be active enough. It speaks more to those whose jobs are in industry, government or the uniformed services, than to the caring and teaching professions. It by no means excludes those who organise, manage or govern these concerns part-time or unpaid. It is natural for such people to seek the satisfaction that comes from a job well done, for we live but once and there may be no second chance. "Whatsoever thy hand findeth to do, do it with thy might; for there is no work . . . in the grave, whither thou goest" (Ecclesiastes 9.10). It is natural to seek approval of one's peers, one's subordinates and if one can get it of one's superiors. But to what extent is it natural, or religiously permissible, to seek the approval of God?

There is clearly one strand of theological opinion which regards any such suggestion as frivolous. All have sinned and fallen short of the standards which God sets. Before him one can only stand in penitence, asking forgiveness, being at best content that by his action sin has been taken away – until we lapse again. Jesus is more positive. In his warning story of the sheep and goats (Matthew 25. 31–46) he teaches that at judgement day the Son of Man will bless and reward those of all nations who have undertaken works of mercy: nourished the hungry and thirsty, taken in strangers, clothed the naked, visited the sick and come to those in prison. For most men and women of action, however, these are spare-time activities, not their ordinary work. St Paul is keen on paid work and urges his readers not to abandon it; whether for evangelism or in expectation of the second coming. But his reasons are unromantically practical: "Study to be quiet, and to do your own business, and to work with your own hands as we commanded you; that you may walk honestly toward them that are without, and that ye may have lack of nothing" (1 Thessalonians 4. 11, 12). The labourer, in other words, is worthy of his hire; if a man would eat, let him work, and not be a charge on the community.

But, there is little sense here of work as an expression *in itself* of Christian vocation. The best example in Christian teaching is Jesus's parable of the talents (Matthew 25. 14–30). Here the Lord heaps praises and promotion upon those servants who, while he was away, have doubled his money by trade. The least able servant, who has hidden his money out of fear of losing it, is upbraided as wicked and slothful. For failing to put the money to the exchangers at usury he is fined and cast into outer darkness: "From him that hath not shall be taken away even that which he hath . . . there shall be weeping and gnashing of teeth." These penalties for the unprofitable are well known, both in the game of *Monopoly* and on the Stock Exchange. But, Jesus was speaking of the Kingdom of Heaven, so what on earth can he have meant?

Jesus was a Jew, and throughout history the Jews have thriven, as some do to this day, by lending money to the powerful, sometimes even at the extortionate rates approved of in the parable. Jesus clearly had nothing against money as such, and accepted financial support from many ladies whom he had healed of psychic or bodily ills (Luke 8. 2,3). But, he taught that it was hard indeed for a rich man to enter the Kingdom, encouraged the wealthy publican Zacchaeus to pay back four times over those whom he had cheated, and cast the traders out of the temple (Luke 18.25; 19.8, 45). So, he can scarcely have intended his parable of the money market to be taken too literally.

Since the fourteenth century the Greek word for money in the parable – talent – has come to mean in English a mental endowment or natural ability, viewed as something divinely entrusted to a person for use and improvement. In line with this usage a modern interpretation of the parable by Fred Catherwood runs as follows:

> It would be fair to deduce from this teaching that it is the duty of the Christian to use his abilities to the limits of his physical and mental capacity. He cannot relax as soon as he has got enough money or as soon as he has mastered his job. He has a duty to train himself and develop his abilities, both academically and experimentally, to the limit that his other responsibilities allow. When he has mastered one job he should go on to another. He should not be content to administer, but should try to improve and innovate. He should not stop until it is quite clear that he had reached his ceiling. . . . The Christian does not work to earn a living; he works because God intended that he should use the gifts he had given him for the fulfilment of divine purpose. . . . No labour is degrading.[1]

This rather ferocious work ethic, while going well beyond what St Paul taught, certainly matches the stark "use it or lose it" tone of the parable. It captures well the spirit of Enterprise Britain, based as it is explicitly on the Victorian paradigm of Samuel Smiles: *Self-Help, Thrift, Character, Duty*. It is not a recipe for unredeemed workaholism; indeed the author emphasises the need to give time and energy to wife and family, and to spiritual devotions. With protestant rigour he insists that no secular affairs should spill over into Sunday. But neither can one claim that this unremitting stress on self-improvement and promotion is explicitly demanded by the gospel. It is certainly quite foreign to most Christian cultures. Even in the context of twenty-first century England there is need for a more nuanced regime. The trend is towards more part-time working, careers better suited to the needs of women, working from home, the need to nurture low-track staff, to recognise the significance of stress, to take account of green concerns. So, the parable can also teach us the highly modern lesson that at a time of talent shortage, those concerns which make the best use of existing staff will have the competitive edge. "It is all down to people."[2]

The emphasis in the parable upon money and promotion, and the resulting double meaning of the English word *talent*, have driven this discussion along the routes of traditional manpower planning: pay, skills and career development. But, there is much more to a job than this. Where the Church has in the past had least to say is in the area of greatest perplexity; that is the content of the work itself. There is an obvious difficulty here. Where technicalities are concerned – how to design or fabricate a component, to provide a resource or frame an argument – there is no substitute for inherited craft and the judgement of peers. These are professional concerns, where there is little room for a distinctively Christian voice. At the higher level of generality the Church can offer re-assurance. It *is* both possible and desirable to run a trading business honestly – although it may by no means be the most profitable. A soldier or police officer *can* be a faithful Christian; and will be all the better for it. But, these are disappointingly obvious.

Archbishop William Temple, sensing the need for middle axioms, giving more detailed guidance at an intermediate level, offered the example of bridge building. It is not the business of the Church, he said, to tell the engineers how to build a bridge, but to remind them of the need to build it safely. In so saying he fell straight into the trap that he himself had spotted. As it happens, to build safely is the one thing of which no bridge builder needs reminding. Every bridge is a compromise between many factors. The three principal ones are: economy of resources (materials, labour, time and cost); robustness (against wind, water, and all the loads that will ever be imposed upon it); and fitness for its setting, not least aesthetically. The point is that engineers owe a professional duty to their clients – and thus if they are Christians to God – in regard to *all* of these factors, and many others, including some of which the client himself may well be unaware. To pick out one of these duties arbitrarily and hold it up as the Christian one is jejune and brings the whole procedure into disrepute.

The concept of middle axioms, detailed enough to be of practical use yet still susceptible to specific Christian valuation, is therefore problematical. It may be that for Christian men and women of action there is more to be gleaned from their religion about the style in which they set about their duties, rather than from guidance as to content. Since for the most part we are concerned with those whose duties are to organise or control, the question of management style is best addressed as leadership. We have in the Church of England a recognised prophet in this field. Professor John Adair's thesis has been set out in many books over the past 20 years.[3] Among his list of core leadership traits he includes such "unfashionable" qualities

as warmth, integrity and enthusiasm. His most recent list of the "seven deadly sins" in business leadership consists of the following:
– Failing to consult people
– Taking people for granted
– Maintaining control through dividing and ruling
– Failing to think through objectives, relying instead on crisis management
– Co-ordinating projects instead of making a personal contribution
– Failing to communicate with staff and listen to their views
– Failing to lead by example.

He emphasises that leadership should exist at every level; a concept which is anti-hierarchical and one which the English, he says, are not yet ready to accept. Its Christian basis is self-evident, stemming from the need to treat every man and woman as of value in their own right. This is a message which speaks very plainly to many of this country's current discontents and we ignore it at our peril.

If it is difficult to discern the role of Christian counsel within any given enterprise or profession, the difficulties multiply at the level of society at large. What was taught in first-century Palestine can self-evidently have little direct application at this level to advanced industrial societies. Writers of equally impeccable Christian credentials arrive at diametrically opposed conclusions. It was in 1848, the year of the *Communist Manifesto*, that two Anglican clerics, the novelist Charles Kingsley and F. D. Maurice, then Professor of Divinity at King's College, London, proclaimed themselves "Christian Socialists" and were reviled by fellow Christians for *Jacobinism and Jacquerie*. Kingsley had asked the damning question "What is the use of preaching about heaven to hungry paupers?" Essentially the same question is raised today by Liberation theologians and the debate continues. Some Christian conservatives would prefer the Church to stick to evangelism, prayer, charity and reminders to their flock to save their souls. But, the Industrial Christian Fellowship, through Kenneth Adams, has reminded us that work within the productive processes, by which life is sustained and wealth created, is also a primary Christian vocation in its own right, and should be affirmed as such. The Archbishop of Canterbury emphasises the corporate dimension to our faith and ethics, an aspect taken for granted in other churches. The social encyclicals of the Roman

Church represent a continuous tradition of analysis, going back centuries, setting out how societies can best organise themselves economically and politically for the greater good, under the insights of faith. The East German protestant churches are arousing admiration by the firm political stance they have taken in exhorting their flocks not to migrate westwards, but imploring their government to entertain dialogue with reformist groups. But, political churchmen make the English uneasy. And, when we turn to the specifics – whether of local government taxation, penal reform, the Great Debate on education, reform of the medical and legal systems, privatisation of water and electricity, immigration, the laws on abortion or genetic engineering – on all of these subjects, while there has been a lively Christian debate there have been no generally agreed conclusions. Are Anglicans to take it that God approves of all work in these fields or of none?

Nor will it do to take refuge in the stratagem which treats all views as Christianly valid provided they are held sincerely. As Ronald Higgins points out:

> Only by acknowledging and weighing our own dark side can we stop fooling ourselves about what we are doing. One of the most insidious and perilous vices in international (as in personal) life is "sincerity" – our truly awful capacity to believe in our own propaganda.[4]

Based upon his work at St James's Piccadilly, Higgins has become aware of a menacing global orthodoxy now infecting, but by no means confined to, the West, supremely unsuited to the gathering crisis of escalating numbers pressing on scarce resources:

> We have an ethic of personal success rather than general welfare; of "loads-a-money" hedonism rather than restraint; of "fast-track" enterprise rather than prudence; of short-term profit rather than long-term benefit; of exploitation rather than conservation; of stimulated wants rather than essential needs; of national pride rather than international responsibility; of rampant individualism ("society doesn't exist") rather than collective obligation.

Christians, confronting these perplexities, have no title to despair. There is need for *metanoia*, repentance, a complete change of direction in public affairs. But nor must Christians fall into the *hubris* of supposing that all can be solved by some colossal strokes of policy. As Herbert Butterfield explained in his Cambridge lectures *Christianity and History*[5], which read today as freshly as when he delivered them 40 years ago, we must avoid the sin of playing too high a game with providence. He quotes two pregnant metaphors of Bismarck:

> The statesman cannot create the stream of time, he can only navigate upon it.

> The statesman must try and reach for the hem when he hears the garment of God rustling through events.

So, the task for men and women of action is clear. It is to find a less arrogant way of co-operating with providence. It is to navigate cautiously, one way-point at a time, making such heading as wind and waves allow. It is to recognise that no course is ever better than a compromise; if it is no more than 50 per cent successful at least it can give a 50 per cent return. It is to have the moral courage to believe that what one is doing is worth doing. It is to listen in case one should hear the rustle of God's garment down the wind. For many it is to be content working away in the engine room without any clear hearing, or vision of how the navigational plot is working out. For all but a very few it is a task of painstaking detail.

> He who would do good to another must do it in Minute Particulars. General Good is the plea of the scoundrel, hypocrite and flatterer. (William Blake)

Sir Hugh Beach served for 40 years in the British Army (Royal Engineers). His last post in the Army was as Master General of the Ordnance (Board member for procurement of land service equipment). Since then he has been for five years Warden of St George's House, Windsor Castle, for three years Director of the Council for Arms Control. He is now chairman of Rochester 2000, the Winchester Diocesan Advisory Council for the Care of Churches, the Gordon Foundation and the Church Army.

Thinking for ourselves

Susan Edwards

Background

ONE OF THE jobs of the Church is to encourage everybody to think for themselves. We have been through a long period when it was unfashionable for people to have ideas of their own; perhaps it has always been so. Man is by nature a social creature and as such, it is essential for there to be leaders, and consequently, those who follow. Whether as king, a commander of troops, a feudal lord or the elected president, someone has to be in control, someone makes the decisions, someone tells the others what they should do. In recent years the Specialist has been held in awe. Society has become so complicated that large areas of it are incomprehensible to the majority so we have encouraged those who will, to take responsibility for us. The Church today is a product both of our history and this current attitude. It used to be that the Church was the social leader, the land-owner, the holder of political power. Although much of that has been lost, we have allowed the clergy to assume our responsibility and become the Specialist in Theology.

Changes

LIFE is played out in a series of circles or wheels, however. And, just as the wheels which made the Church rich and powerful have turned, so the willingness of people to be directed is also turning. This is often seen as a threat, a challenge to the authority of the Church, especially by the insecure, but it can also be a tremendous opportunity to realise the vision of the Church as the *whole* people of

25

God. The days of clergy telling parishioners what they should think or believe are coming to an end. Praise the Lord, for he gives us all free will. Of course, there are still many who would prefer to be told what it is they believe, who would rather not face the challenge of discovering for themselves the wondrous nature of faith, nor the obligation of deciding for themselves how to express it. In this they are aided and abetted by many a vicar; but at last there are signs that we are being moved on. Within the confines of the parish, new life is struggling to be born, as indeed it is in the world at large. There are many areas where people are assuming accountability for the future of humanity and the world.

God's call to his people

IN 1 Peter 2.9ff, Christians are described as "a chosen people, a royal priesthood, a holy nation, a people belonging to God". The first part of this quotation is well known and often quoted, but the second part gives the purpose for choosing the people: "that you may declare the praises of him who *called you* out of darkness into his wonderful light". It goes on: "Once you were not a people, but now you are the people of God." It is not only Jews that are addressed here. Its relevance for Christians today is as real as when it was written. The Church must recognise its importance and significance and act accordingly. We are the people of God, he calls *us*. This means that it is not the role of the clergy to take total responsibility for their congregations. Nor is it enough for them to condescend to share it with the laity of their choice; responsibility belongs to all the people of God the *laos, all* called, *all* chosen to be part of the royal priesthood, included in the holy nation, belonging to the God who gave us free will: as Christians, we have chosen to use that free will to be his people. It is the clergy's task to enable us to help one another. As St Paul puts it, we each have our individual load to carry, but we must also carry each other's burdens. (Galatians 6.2,5). The title of this book, *Building in Love*, gives us an image of the Church being built. Building is a continuous process, one which must never stop, and which must be done with great care and much love. If it continues to grow in one area only, or stops in another, the *whole building* will become unstable. All areas of the Church need building up. The sooner the Church gives up treating congregations as flocks of sheep and recognises them as groups of *people* answering God's call, the sooner they will respond accordingly.

Which Christians can grow through thinking?

GROUPS of people are made up of individuals – so true and yet so easy to overlook. It is popular to categorise people, and often the categories are paired – men/women; old/young; clergy/laity; intelligent/stupid; healthy/sick; and now – "those who think"/"those who don't". Congregations are made up of all these categories mixed together, although each will have a larger percentage of one than another but be sure that there is no-one who *cannot* think. The Church's task is to encourage people to think, to think about God, to think "theologically" and to express this thinking in their living. This involves encouraging the whole *laos* to develop and use a gift they already have – the gift of thought. We are those to whom God gave free will – let us use it, but let us ensure that we are given as much help, information and encouragement as we each need to make our choices wisely. As Christians, we are the body of Christ on earth, so must grow and build each other up, each part doing its work.

On what shall we think? – the vision

PART of this process involves vision, for without vision there can be no growth. Proverbs 29.18a: "Where there is no vision, the people perish." This is from the King James version; others translate "the people perish" as – "go astray", "are without order", "run wild", "cast off restraint". Throughout history, where the people have had no vision they have indeed gone astray, behaved without order, run wild, cast off restraint. Our present times are certainly no exception. Lack of self-control, and the accompanying loss of any sense of self-worth, shows itself in the widespread use of drugs, in world-wide pollution, irresponsible use of chemicals, reckless consumption of resources, appalling weapons and man's inhumanity to man. Only as the vision is recaptured will there be any hope. The vision here is of oneness with God accomplished through his gifts of salvation and resurrection, of Life, which springs from his identification with his creation, and his guidance for it. If we cannot see the truth of the vision, we will perish. If we cannot see a glimmer of what his plan for our future may be, we have no future.

The Church, and we must realise that includes *all* Christians, has the awesome responsibility of convincing people that God's vision as we see it in Jesus, is a vision of fullness of life for all. We are to recapture this vision and live it. Bring the vision out and let the people see it! I believe that already people are seeking the vision; they may not know what it is they are looking for, nor even where to look, but they are beginning. Almost everywhere there are signs of people seeking life's meaning, not just for themselves, but for their neighbours, even for the environment. So many are wanting to do something good, wanting to help those who are less fortunate, wanting "something" but not knowing "what". They are being called and are trying to respond, but do not understand what they hear. Look around and see how many there are who try one religion after another, and others who seek fulfilment in work, drugs, alcohol, sport, danger, violence – all seeking for a meaning for their existence. In Christ, Christians have the key to fullness of life but have to put that key into the hands of the lost, the weary and the weak, the young, the strong and the enthusiastic, so that God's power and glory may be seen in all their splendour.

The structure needed to help Christians to think and grow

IF PEOPLE are to grow as thinkers, they need the right structure in which to grow. This is true for all Christians: they have made a commitment, they need to be helped to keep it. There are two ways of looking at the way we live – either as a series of endings or as a series of beginnings. Take, as an example, confirmation preparation: this can be seen as an end in itself, a fixed period when a particular topic is studied in depth, ending with the special event – confir-

PLEASE KEEP THIS
FOR YOUR RECORDS

PLEASE KEEP THIS
FOR YOUR RECORDS

16:33   28/12/88   :
AUTH CODE:44592
CUSTOMER NOT PRESENT
AR MOWBRAY & CO
28 MARGARET ST LONDON W1
02420224,1951   0558866

VISA
4121740160400534
0389   KEYED

THANK YOU
£38.30

- - - - - - - - - - - - - - -

mation. I believe that the Church must give a more positive view and teach the confirmation as a "beginning", not an isolated happening. As the service ends, so a new stage begins, a new person emerges. If the erstwhile candidate is to continue to grow in Christian faith, there must be a framework which is strong enough to give support, but flexible enough to allow growth in whichever direction is best for them. (This applies equally to all Christians, however long ago they made their commitment.) Visualise the Church itself as this framework – not a cage which restricts and confines thinking, but a trellis encouraging and allowing growth both upward and outward. The strength of the Church lies in its structure. It is this which enables Christians who are physically removed from the structure, for example by imprisonment or oppression, to continue in spiritual growth despite their isolation. They know that they are part of it even though they may not be able to communicate with it, they can feel it even though they cannot see it. Although, at times, it is the size of the structure which appears to be its strength, in reality it lies in the flexibility of thought permitted by its unity of purpose. It was the unity of purpose which held the early Church together as it struggled to develop, its flexibility of thought which enabled it to grow even in times of hardship or persecution, providing unity and support for the whole. We must ensure that the structure today is equally flexible yet supportive.

The growth of the Christian as thinker through the use of authority

TO THE CHRISTIAN there is no doubting the authority of God. But when we accept his authority over us, we then find he has given it back to us. He trusts us to use it wisely. Those who have been given a position of authority in the Church have tremendous opportunities for encouraging the growth of Christians as thinkers. They must use their authority wisely, and this may mean much more boldly than expected, or more gently than their personal inclination would demand. The Church must use its authority to widen the horizons of Christians; use it to give them more opportunities for exploration of what it means to be a part of the Church, to be one more vital link in a continuous line of people seeking to live out the vision, a people who stretch back and who stretch out into the future. Those who have authority must use it to encourage and enable others to develop and use their own authority. Some will have authority over others, some need to accept authority for themselves. For example, if one has authority for worship, use it to give others as varied a range of experience as possible; let them worship using the old liturgies, using the new, then help them to write their own – a liturgy which uses their own language, their own natural style of thinking and speaking; help them to appreciate why and how our public services of worship are the way they are, encourage them to participate where they can, let them *explore worship* and experience it in all its fullness. Be careful, use the authority wisely, be bold in outlook, but sensitive to the fears of the congregation; when they are ready be prepared to make changes. If there is a need, encourage people to recognise it and accept authority themselves for meeting that need. Always support them, but let them make their own discoveries. Encourage them to explore their relationship with God through prayer: to think about different ways of praying, aids to prayer, meditative prayer, to pray themselves, help them to experience God and to recognise him speaking, not only as interpreted for them by their clergy or group leader, but *directly to them*. The hardest part of accepting authority is to give it away.

Growth of the Christian as a thinker through experience

THERE CAN NEVER be a point at which anyone can say: "Enough, I know everything I need to know about God." Always we must go on trying to discover more about him, about his vision, his will for us. We must go on praising, worshipping, praying, listening, communicating. Christians can never be satisfied with their position. To be a Christian is total commitment for life, in order to gain Life. There must be continual seeking after knowledge, truth, guidance and experience of God. Experience leads to change and growth. If we are to continue to grow in faith, we need continually to experience God in our lives. It is through experience that we learn best. If we are told something we may learn *about* it, but something which has been experienced is *known*. Experience changes us; it may cause us to turn away and grow inward or we may meet the challenge of the experience and blossom. It all depends on how we think about it, on the support we get in helping us to find the spiritual dimension: to find God in our experience and, having found him, to grow. "Ordinary" Christians often have very little idea of their strengths or capabilities. The Church must guide them, not restrict them by only using special religious or archaic language in relation to God; free them from inherited inhibitions of status or role – either their own or that of the clergy; not ridicule or dismiss their ideas, but always encourage and help them to realise their potential. *All people think* – tell them so. Make sure that they think about growing as a Christian. Christianity is not just about God seeking to give us salvation, but about demanding our response, our commitment to him in return. Awareness of this does not come all at once, automatically, when people become Christians, but needs to be explained and worked at: show them, lead them, encourage them to think – then let them choose their own response. Some responses have elements in common, but everyone has something of their own to offer, we must share experiences. Often it is only when putting a personal experience into words for another to share that one becomes aware of aspects of its importance and how it has caused change and growth.

The first Christians as thinkers

TO BE A CHRISTIAN is to be a follower of Christ; and in becoming a follower to want to be as like him as it is possible for each one of us to be. Christ on earth, in human form, was the first and last person to be truly as God intended humanity – and, in being fully human, he was *whole*. In his wholeness he was at once one with both his humanity and God. Throughout the gospels we can read of his growth in self-awareness, of his growth in awareness of his relationship with God, and his growth in realisation of his mission. All these aspects of his life were inextricable, and, as he changed in one area, the others were affected too. There are many instances in the bible of his working at changing his disciples too, encouraging them to notice things about themselves that had changed, encouraging them to *think* and to realise the change that accepting God into their lives and giving themselves to his service had made to them. It was their eventual acceptance of this realisation that made them his disciples, those to whom Jesus entrusted his mission. The process of change, thinking and awareness continued throughout their whole ministry, and they needed and gave constant support and guidance to each other. Sometimes the early Christians were unaware of change and then they made mistakes, they did not grow in Christianity, but away from it. Much of the content of St Paul's letters is guidance to Christians who have changed without growth in self-awareness and so grown away from Christ or were in danger of doing so. 2 Peter 3.16ff tells of the difficulty of understanding the content of some of Paul's letters unless one were a Christian, but urging the recipients to persevere and think about them so that they would not fall away from Christianity and salvation. Such encouragement and guidance is still needed if we are to continue to grow in faith. We must always remember that we are all members of one Church and so must consider each other. Clergy need to change and grow too and should be ready to accept help from fellow Christians – whether lay or ordained; It is an unhealthy Church whose laity expect their clergy to remain the same or whose clergy are complacent about the lack of change in their congregations. Those who lead must do precisely that, not by assuming an air of self-sufficiency but of humility, showing by their example the need for accepting guidance. As individuals change and grow in faith, so the whole Church will reflect those changes and grow too. In 1 Corinthians 14, Paul exhorts the church in Corinth to think and consider what they are doing, and consider whether it is helpful to their growth as Christians: verse 20: "Brothers, stop thinking like children – in your thinking be adults" i.e. be responsible and aware.

Thinking about "self" – the growth of the Christian through self-awareness

CHRIST is in us – if we are unaware of ourselves we are unaware of Christ at his closest. For any of us to become one with God, we have first to become aware of "who we are". As Christians we have a very special relationship with God. Through prayer, worship, study etc. we try to build that relationship up. Yet, if we are unaware of our own uniqueness, of our own self, we cannot build. It is impossible to make a relationship with someone you don't know, or who hides important facets of their nature; how then can anyone make a relationship between God and self, if the self is unknown? Interaction with another causes change and growth. As we grow in our relationship with God, we are changed by and through the relationship. We need to be aware of the changes, both in ourselves, and in others as they grow. If we are unaware of the change we are denying God's influence in our lives. Both as a body and as individuals within the body, the Church must encourage and support the growth of Christianity through the growth of its own awareness of what it is we are about – being the body of Christ on earth.

What does the Church do with the Christians it has encouraged to think?

THERE IS no point in the Church encouraging "thinkers" if they are not listened to. Once the awareness of the individual Christian has been stirred, it is important both to that person and to the whole Church that the awareness is channelled into building up the whole Church. Each must be given the opportunity to use new-found gifts. Christians must serve the Church, – the whole body – not create a Church which will serve the chosen few who presume to know God's will. It is God, working through his Holy Spirit who has called, and to deny Christians the opportunity to answer the call is to deny God. We cannot know his plan for his creation.

There is no point in the Church encouraging people only to *think* about theology. The future of the Church depends on all Christians being able to think on God to their individual best, with all their being, at all times, in every aspect of their lives. The fulfilment of the body of Christ on earth depends on the fulfilment of every part of the body. Fulfilment comes through awareness. The Church *must* concentrate on how we can encourage people to think in order to increase their awareness of themselves, of God and of his vision, and how they can become part of the vision. Neither clergy nor intelligent laity have all the answers, all Christians can and must learn from each other. We must always remember that *God is the initiator* and so there is no hiding from our responsibility to those who ask the questions, and seek the answers. In fact we must rejoice simply because there *are* always questions which cannot be answered, for this is a sign of God's greatness – we can never, in this life, know all the answers.

We must never stop asking questions, never stop trying to learn, never stop thinking: never stop giving God the opportunity to communicate with us through our thinking.

Susan Edwards, a former student on the St Albans Ministerial Training Scheme, is now a parish administrator and author.

A pattern of pastoral ministry

W. H. Vanstone

THE PARISH to which I went 40 years ago as curate was as tightly packed with people as any district that I have ever known. It was a product of the third quarter of the nineteenth century – street upon street of small terraced houses built for occupation by the crowds of workers who were then coming from far and near to serve in the ever-multiplying cotton mills of Lancashire. The objective of the builders was obviously that the workers should live as close as possible to the mills: so the houses were built to take up a minimum of space. The front door of virtually every house opened directly onto the street: and behind each house there was a stone-flagged yard no more than a few metres square. Even in my day there, a hundred years after the building began, the only trees in the parish were two black poplars and an old hawthorn in the small garden of the vicarage, and the only open spaces were the asphalted yards of minimum size beside the schools. The church, which dated from some 15 years after the building began, was so tightly hemmed in by houses that, being quite lofty, it gave the impression of a ship moored in dry dock.

I arrived at the parish in the autumn: and in the winter evenings which followed I felt the contrast between the monotony and drabness of the gas-lit streets along which I walked and the rich variety of human activity which was going on so close to me behind the walls and curtains of scores and hundreds of houses. On the pavements I was never more than three or four feet from someone's living room: and when I visited a house I would step directly from the dismal and usually empty street into the very heart of the life of a person or a family – and there almost anything might be going on, from a family quarrel to the bathing of a new-born baby, from an eager game

35

among children to the tending of a dying invalid. I came to think of the long, dismal wall of a row of houses as no more than a facade which was concealing behind it an extraordinary richness and variety of human activity and experience.

I am sure that what I felt as I walked the streets had been felt long before my time by clergy of the parish, and that it had much to do with the pattern and standard of pastoral ministry which was both expected and practised there. During the 80 years that the church had then existed there had been only three vicars – of whom the third, my own vicar, had been brought up in the parish. So there was firm continuity of memory and practice: and it was evident from what I heard of the past that the remarkable pastoral diligence of my own vicar had been characteristic of his two predecessors also. I believe that in each of them it was rooted in his sensitivity to the rich and highly-charged human potential which was throbbing and pulsating behind the monotonous facades of the tightly packed streets.

All these three men were totally convinced that "this was where the action was". None of them had any thought of promotion or a change of scene, and all of them kept their extra-parochial activities to the barest minimum. They were constantly up and down the streets of the parish on foot: and I was often told of my vicar's predecessor that he was still up and down the streets even when, in an advanced stage of Parkinson's disease, he had to use the walls for support or knock himself against them to effect a change of direction. It was not, I think, heroic self-denial that kept these men so faithful to pastoral ministry in their parish: it was the cool intellectual conviction that no other work or charge could possibly be more important than the work which they did and the charge which they held.

These three men were also convinced that the dynamic human potential of the parish could not be adequately developed and fulfilled within the narrow limits of each of the small houses. Private life in the homes and families of the district needed, for its own healthy development, the outlet and enrichment of life in community. So from the early days of the church it had been pastoral policy to create and sustain such an outlet. Since there was no open space in the parish the first vicar obtained from a local magnate the gift of a field just outside the parish: and long before my time this had been developed by the church into a fine sports' ground with football pitch, tennis courts, changing rooms and so on. There had also been developed long before my time a multitude of clubs, societies and shared activities for which the church schools were used in the evenings and at weekends. The variety of these clubs and activities was remarkable – from holiday savings club to dramatic society: from football club to weekly whist drives and dances: from lectures and handicraft classes for men and women to the bands and camps and manifold physical activities of the uniformed organisations for boys and girls. On an average evening at least half a dozen organised activities would be going on in the schools: and on summer evenings another two or three groups would be active on the sports' ground.

Participation in these clubs was by no means restricted to church members or professing Christians: it was wide open to all the parish. There was even a club, with the extraordinary and self-chosen name of "the Nobodies", for boys of the streets who did not want to be associated with the church. But all these clubs were promoted by the church, had free use of church land and premises and were led and managed by people of the church. The phrase "lay ministry" was not yet fashionable in the days of my curacy: but in fact, of course, a very effective and extensive ministry was then being carried on by the lay people who held the key positions in these clubs. For it was taken for granted that these people were responsible not only for the good management and financial probity of the clubs but also for the pastoral care of their members. It was accepted that if a member were "missing" or behaved in an unusual way a responsible official of the club should "follow him up" or "see what was troubling her". Even a "difficult" member of the Scouts or the Dramatic Society must not be allowed simply to "drift away". So a remarkable amount of timely but quite unselfconscious lay ministry went on in that parish: when the Guide Captain called because a girl had been absent for a fortnight she might find that the parents were deeply troubled by their daughter's behaviour, and when the secretary of the football club went round to see if a player had got over his injury on Saturday he might well be told that, though the footballer was all right, his father or mother was seriously ill.

This particular layman, the secretary of the football club for many years and later churchwarden also, exemplified at an almost saintly level the lay ministry of the parish. At work he never rose above the status of labourer and he never married. In his young days he had been a brilliant footballer of professional standard and all through life he retained his enthusiasm for the game. But even football came second in his eyes to the needs and distresses of sick and lonely people. To them he devoted all his spare time when he was working and, after he retired from work, virtually all his time. For hours each day he was up and down the streets on his rounds of practical service – helping a cripple to dress, lighting an old woman's fire, shaving the victim of a stroke, taking someone out in a wheel-chair, going errands or just "calling in" to see that someone was all right. Through his experience he became a remarkably skilful nurse: he is the only person I have ever known who, when he visited someone in hospital, was on occasion asked by the nurses to give a patient a bedpan or a bath or a shave. In his mid-seventies he collapsed and died in the street on his way to give an old man a shave. His funeral was attended by over 600 people – virtually all from the parish.

I remember vividly the phrases in which this quiet and lovely man would sometimes report one of his charges to the vicar: "Bill Smith, 27 East Street . . . had a stroke . . . don't think you'll know him – he hasn't been here long . . . I go each night and he's all right . . . but you'll go, won't you?" And then, equally briefly, he would tell the vicar the particular reason why he should "go": "he's getting near the end" or "he says he's an unbeliever" or "he's fallen out with his daughter". And, of course, the vicar would "go".

For this was the accepted role of the vicar – to be, as the recognised representative of the church as a whole, a kind of back-up to the pastoral work of lay-people. He did not organise or supervise their work, or call them to meetings or ask for reports: he simply kept close to them, calling in for a few minutes on each of the clubs at least once in every two or three weeks and relying on the leaders to tell him, there and then or at any other time, of any matters which were seriously affecting the lives of their members. He trusted their good sense to tell him what he ought to know; and, as far as I can remember now, his trust was rarely unjustified. For the lay leaders could and did trust him. If they told him that one of their members was in hospital, or that his or her marriage was on the rocks, or that so-and-so had adopted a child he would "follow up" what he was told with a visit in a matter of hours rather than days. It was clear that he took, with serious and competent professionalism, his duty as the representative of the church to bring himself very close to parishioners at times of change or crisis or decision in their lives. He did not wait for them to come to him: he went to them, knowing that it is at such times that people tend to take an important step either towards God or away from him, and that the presence or absence of the church at such times may be decisive for the direction in which the step is taken.

So the diligent pastoral work of the church had a quiet but continuing "evangelistic" spin-off. A visit, whether by lay person or vicar, could in itself be "good news" to parents embarrassed by a child's misbehaviour, to a wife whose husband was in prison or a single person who felt alone in the world. A courteous visit to one's home was a mark of acceptance: and what was said quite naturally in the course of a visit could open more widely the door to faith in God and understanding of the church. As a newcomer to the parish I was often told in the course of my own visiting how a certain person or family "started going to church": and the stories I was told were not of missions or evangelistic campaigns but of how good the football club had been to an errant son or what a comfort the vicar had been when a daughter was dying. Even when I visited people who did not "go to church", I found myself "entering into the labours of others": for I always found the church respected and myself made welcome, and often enough was told, courteously and apologetically, "how it is that I don't go". The past labours of the church, in its clubs and its pastoral ministry, had won for it, at the very least, the unselfconscious respect of the whole parish, and, through that respect, a kind of predisposition in favour of what it taught and stood for. What the church was doing was a continuing and vigorous *praeparatio evangelica* in the parish: and I recall a remark about my vicar's predecessor that, although he did not shine in the pulpit, he preached the gospel very effectively with his feet.

So pastoral and evangelistic work merged into one. And so also did physical and spiritual work. In the saintly figure of the football secretary whom I have mentioned there was a living example of the two made wholly one. In the depth and faithfulness of his service to the sick "the spiritual" was as evident as in his presence at the altar before he began his rounds. So I began to see the truth of a theological principle which I had heard expounded by Paul Tillich only a few months before I came to the parish. I had spent a year in New York sitting at Tillich's feet for five or six hours a week and marvelling at the range of his learning and the power of his theological exposition: and now, in the totally different ambience of a Lancashire parish, I seemed to see some of his major principles put into practice. For Tillich taught *in primis* that "the spiritual" is not a particular area or enclave of reality but the deepest dimension of all reality: that the spiritual is to be discerned not in certain distinct and specific things and activities but in the dimension of depth which is present in all things and all activities.

Tillich believed that the Spirit is the God-given drive which animates all life and which in man inspires all his purposeful activity. Essentially, this driving-force is good: it might almost be described as the aspiration or the return-journey of the Spirit towards the Father and the Son whence he proceeds. But, "in existence" – which was Tillich's phrase for what most of us would call "this fallen world" – this essentially "good" drive can become misdirected, perverted or distorted. It can become so distorted as to be "demonic". Existential distortion is to be forestalled, rectified or healed only through the grace and power of the "new being which is manifested in Jesus as the Christ": and this power must be mediated, made known and available in existence, through "structures of grace". Tillich's terminology was all his own: but in the range and comprehensiveness of his thinking there was a notable "catholicity". He believed that all life is of God, energised by the dynamic of the Spirit: and therefore he would have shared with my vicar and his predecessors their respect for the concentration of human energies which was contained within their tightly-packed parish. He would also have shared their perception that these energies would *either* be distorted into quarrels within families, feuds between families and even gang warfare, *or* find outlet and expression in the kind of shared and corporate activity which draws people who live close to one another into neighbourliness and community. Tillich would have recognised the "clubs" of the church as important "structures" for the achieving of this latter purpose.

I think that, on account of the pastoral ministry which developed from and through them, Tillich would also have recognised them as authentic "structures of grace". For the deeper the human situation to which that ministry attended the more clearly and explicitly the ministry made known and available "the power of the new being in Jesus as the Christ". I continually noticed throughout my curacy that Tillich's highly intellectual and abstract principles were constantly being "earthed" in the pastoral practice of the parish. If the Guide Captain found on a visit that a girl had been absent simply on account of a cold or extra homework then her visit brought simply the good good news that "she had been missed": and the matter would go no further. But, if the absence had been due to meningitis or shame that her father was in prison, then the vicar, having been told of the situation, would very soon "follow it up": and then, as it were, the scene would be set quite naturally for talk with the girl or her parents about shame and forgiveness and death and hope and the healing and saving power of Christ. The diligence and depth of pastoral ministry turned useful organisational structures into authentic structures of grace.

I am writing of pastoral practice in a parish which, even 40 years ago, was judged by some of my contemporaries to be old fashioned and out of date. Even then one was hearing that pastoral visiting was an impossible burden for parish priests and that parishioners should come to them by appointment if they wanted their counsel or comfort: that parochial clergy should give their attention not so much to parishioners as to the "power-structures" of the district, such as the Town Councillors or the Trade Union officials: that the church should concern itself not with the private joys and agonies which keep people awake at night but with public issues which are discussed in the newspapers and the other media: that the church should restrict its interest in the parish to those who are "real" or "committed" Christians or at least show signs of being "trainable" for its purposes. Sometimes Tillich was referred to as an advocate, at least by implication, of such new styles of ministry. I am sure that he was not: for, as an existentialist, he taught that it is at the deeply *personal* level of human experience that the drive of the Spirit becomes misdirected and distorted or rectified or healed. He spoke much of the "boundary situation" of despair or "ecstasy" as the point at which "truth" is lost or grasped: and he showed us with marvellous insight how the boundary situation may present itself in the "ordinary" situations of loneliness, rejection, fear of death, being in love, success, acceptance, the making or breaking of a marriage. I was deeply impressed to find in the parish that it was upon these situations among parishioners that the pastoral endeavour of the church was steadily and faithfully directed.

I was also encouraged that a teacher so "prophetic" as Tillich, so widely recognised for his understanding of the "way the world was going", should be validating in his teaching the practice of this old-fashioned parish. It was evident that the old-fashioned was not necessarily out of date. Forty years later, I still fail to see that pastoral ministry as it was practised in that parish is out of date. Of course, society has greatly changed since the days when Tillich was lecturing in New York and my vicar walking the gas-lit streets of Lancashire; but pastoral principles, objectives and even methods do not necessarily become obsolete with changes in society.

For it must be remembered that the parish of which I write had not always been there: three generations before my time it had been a "new housing estate" to which people moved from far and near to work in the local mills. As such it was a no more "natural" or "promising" setting for a new church than are some of the new estates and tower-blocks of working class housing of to-day: and it contained similar problems of poverty and deprivation. So the pattern of pastoral ministry which the first incumbent established there is not obviously inappropriate in similar areas to-day: and of course there are parishes where it is still being followed vigorously and faithfully. I know for instance of an inner-city parish of the most "deprived" kind in which the vicar's wife, herself the mother of seven children, pays a visit to every mother in the parish who bears a child: of others where the range of church "clubs" and activities is as comprehensive as in the parish of my curacy and generates the same comprehensive knowledge of the parish and the same follow-up of pastoral care: and of course of many another where the vicar is to be seen about the streets as frequently and regularly as was my own vicar.

But there are many parishes where pastoral care appears to be restricted to those who either are members of the congregation at church or have problems or needs which are distinctively "spiritual". One reason for this is that the church as the "worshipping community" has relatively little knowledge of, or contact with, the parish outside that community. Church "clubs" are almost non-existent: and the reason for this is the belief that social needs are being fully met and social activities being made readily available by a multitude of agencies other than the church – from the social services with their clubs for the disabled to the local sports centre with its squash and swimming clubs. Now there is, of course, much truth in this, at least in most districts: and it would be wrong for the church to use its energies in setting up its own clubs to compete for membership with others in the locality. But "special need clubs" and "special interest groups" are not, in themselves, creative of *local* community. They tend to draw members from far and wide and to detach them from, rather than relate them to, the people among whom they live. They are not conducive to "neighbourliness" – to easy relationships with those who happen to live close at hand. It is in our great cities with their multitude of facilities for social activity that multitudes find themselves most isolated and lonely.

So the church, locally based, locally led, with a comprehensive responsibility for that geographical area which is the parish, is still called upon to win districts into communities – to weave around itself that network of natural connections which was created by the clubs of the parish of my curacy. Even parishes inhabited exclusively by stockbrokers need playgroups for little children, service groups for the elderly, local conservation groups, local history groups – groups drawn from the locality simply on the basis of common residence in the locality and promoting that awareness of "belonging together" which is of the essence of neighbourliness and local community. A church which takes the lead in creating and sustaining local community is, by that in itself, proving the value of the parochial system; and, if its leadership is exercised with Christian responsibility, then there will develop, almost inevitably, an ever widening pastoral ministry in the parish.

For the leadership of the church in creating and sustaining local community will be exercised by "lay ministers" – not under that title but under the name of "chairman", "scout leader", "convener", "team leader", "secretary" or whatever it may be; and their ministry will be expressed *both* in the diligence and competence with which they manage the activities of a group *and* the unpretentious pastoral care which they show for its members. They will notice absences and follow them up with a friendly enquiry: and so there will grow in the church a widening knowledge of parishioners outside the worshipping community and of matters and concerns which affect them personally.

This knowledge must be handled responsibly. The church must not become, or seem to become, a gossip-shop. In the parish of my curacy the leaders of the clubs told the vicar, and only the vicar, of serious situations in the lives and homes of their members of which they had become aware. Even the curate was rarely told directly: it was by the vicar that I was asked to visit a certain house and told something of the situation there. I was myself responsible for one particular club, and I would visit the homes of its members at my own discretion; but, when serious matters came to light, I would report them to the vicar so that they should have their appropriate place and priority in the total scheme and system of pastoral care.

That tightly-packed parish was relatively small in area; so its population of about 9000 was no more than about average for a parish. But, over three generations, its pastoral outreach had become so extensive that the number of visits required of the vicar in a week would be around 40. Visiting occupied virtually all his afternoons and the majority of his evenings. But he never spoke of it as a "burden". It fed rather than restricted his ministry as a whole. It gave relevance to his preaching and, I imagine, motive and substance to his prayer. It gave to his advice the authority of a wide experience of people. And, in my casual talk with him, it was the source of endless humour. What is more, as I have already said, it created, in concert with the visiting of the club leaders, a quiet but continuing evangelistic "input" into a very large proportion of the houses of the parish.

It was essential to this evangelistic input that the vicar – and the lay ministers – actually *went* to people, irrespective of who they were, at times of possible or actual pastoral need. They did not simply hold themselves available at certain times for consultation or advice: they took the positive step of "going". They did not go aggressively or demandingly: they offered their presence to people rather than imposed it on them. Possibly in the early days of the parish some parishioners felt threatened, irritated or embarrassed by the presence of "someone from the church" on the doorstep: and, possibly, in parishes where the church is new or where there has been little pastoral visiting in the past, the same may be true today. But diligence in visiting gradually erodes these difficulties. Except for those areas where the majority of people are firm adherents of a different religion, no parishes are "unvisitable" by the church; and I remain firmly convinced of the truth that I learned 40 years ago – that the parishes are "where the action is" and the visiting of parishioners is both a primary duty of the church and a continuing source and safeguard of its own integrity and health and strength.

W. H. Vanstone is a Canon residentiary of Chester Cathedral.

Those outside the Church today

Bill Kirkpatrick

Reaching out

"EARL'S COURT is similar to any inner-city area, a kind of desert, where many come for a whole variety of reasons; for example, the anonymity it offers. Yet, this same anonymity is the source of much loneliness and depression. People, however transient or long-stay, are often cheated through exorbitant prices and poor accommodation facilities. There are several poor-quality bed-and-breakfast hostels; food costs are higher than in many other areas and therefore non-nourishing convenience foods are consumed all too often; recreation facilities are practically nil; it is one of the blackest spots of unemployment in London. The area is unhealthy from every aspect: physically because of environmental pollution, mentally because of the inherent isolation; socially because of its transient nature; spiritually, because spiritual needs are not being sufficiently met. Earl's Court is one of the most crowded places in Europe. The 8,500 members of an ever-changing population with over ninety nationalities, living within half a square mile, appear to be lost as a community. Prostitution, both male and female, is a major concern. Equally so are the problems of alcohol and drug abuse, addiction and overdose. The substantially large gay population, by its very presence, is also part of our total concern within the area."

With these words, Bill Kirkpatrick describes the world where he has worked and lived as a priest since 1979. He believes the Church needs to evolve a more concrete vision of a "cellular ministry" in its mission towards the inhabitants of all the "Earl's Courts" of society.

Trevor Huddleston describes his achievement: "As each year passes it is clear that the special ministry of Father Bill Kirkpatrick is indeed "reaching out" to more and more people. Behind a whole area, a whole population, lies the tragedy of deprivation: of a poverty and therefore a need which is a challenge to all Christians and indeed to all who care at all about the future of our civilisation. Thank God for those who, like Bill Kirkpatrick, are called to meet that challenge with such commitment and compassion."

The reader will inevitably ask what *is* Bill Kirkpatrick's work, what does he actually *do*, who *are* the "outsiders" he reaches?

A listening service

"MY JOB DESCRIPTION," he says, "is to be a listener. Everything else is secondary to and follows on from that. I came to Earl's Court simply to be in the area and listen to people. I realised this was where the holy spirit was moving me. That was in 1979. The then bishop of London said I could do what I liked, with his blessing, but that I'd have to find the money. I found a flat and went to a Trust to ask for support. It must have sounded peculiar, to say 'I need financial assistance in order to listen'. The Trust members may have wondered whether they were going to get value for their money. Fortunately, they decided they were. They bought the flat, and here I came to live.

"For the first six months I saw no one at all. I was beginning to be convinced I had made a mistake and that no one was ever going to turn up. Then I started going into the pubs and clubs in the neighbourhood and began to know faces. Initially, I used to go in without a clerical collar and that didn't work too well. Some people were looking for a 'sugar daddy' – I might have looked like one, but I certainly didn't have the sugar – and then I began to go with a collar on. It felt less deceitful. I was there as a priest. Gradually, people started to talk to me. The combination of the collar and the cross I wear round my neck made connections – the cross because it's an unusual one and people want to know what it is and where it comes from.

"After talking to someone I might say, 'Here's my card. I live round the corner. If you want to turn up sometime, you're welcome.' I reckon about 10% do, but maybe a month or so later. At first, I'm simply being tested out. I see all manner of people, from senior citizens who need someone to chat with to severely damaged people, people who feel like committing suicide and – increasingly – people from the gay community, some of whom are infected with and those affected by the AIDS virus, and young persons who have become involved, for a whole variety of reasons, in prostitutional activities. Frequently, most have not been treated too well by the Church and they have to decide whether to bother with me, because I'm obviously part of the establishment whether I like it or not.

"When people do turn up I try to listen in such a way that they will hear themselves and know that the answers to their problems come from deep within themselves and not from my saying what they should or should not do. I don't like the term 'spiritual director'. I prefer 'soul friend', someone who walks alongside others at their speed, from where they happen to be but examining together where they might be heading. Naturally, I make suggestions, but I never instruct: 'Do this, that or the other!' The first thing for the persons I might help is to be comfortable with me, next being comfortable with themselves. Then, they will begin to understand who they are and where they are going."

A ministry to those infected with and affected by HIV/AIDS

"ABOUT FIVE YEARS AGO I received a phone call from the Terence Higgins Trust asking me to go and see someone who was dying of AIDS. They couldn't find a priest who was prepared to go. I did, and was launched into a whole new area of mission. It's not just a ministry to those who are infected with the virus, but also to those who are affected by it, the sufferers' lovers and their families. All need care, in differing ways. In these five years, at times, I've been burying someone every ten days. That's a privilege, but a heavy load on the psyche. The circumstances are often difficult. There are the parents who didn't know that their son was gay, or had a lover, and when they hear their son is dying their immediate reaction is to say it's the lover's fault. It's natural to blame somebody when your life is shattered by the premature death of a son or daughter. It's important, though, to begin to heal that pain by not being judgemental.

At the other extreme there are parents on both sides who know the full story, where each family reckon they have gained a son.

"I think AIDS is a universal syndrome for a universal viral infection, that knows no boundaries. In a sense the Church has got HIV/AIDS! Every baptised person is a member of the Church, many baptised persons have AIDS, so what is the Church doing? I regret she remains frightened, still, of the body, and of the gift of our sexualities. My hope is that one good thing that may come out of the presence of AIDS in the world is that the Church will look anew at the gift of sexuality and recognise its *co*-creative potential, and not just its *pro*-creative potential. When two people love each other, whether it's expressed sexually or not, their job is to enable each other to grow. Where that is happening, how can we be judgemental? And judgemental about a virus at that! We don't judge the common cold – but that's because we're not afraid of it."

Dying

BUT, Bill Kirkpatrick believes, it's not only sexuality that the Church needs to look at afresh, but dying. "We know we're going to die but we don't look at it in relation to our lives. Yet, whenever we make a major change, we have died. But people, in the Church and outside, don't look at and interpret their lives in terms of death and rebirth. When I am attempting to care for young people who are shortly to die, I approach them in this way: 'This isn't the end' is my message. 'The centre of all things is God. God is love, and God will embrace you whatever you believe and however you have got there. If the Church finds it difficult embracing you, God won't, because God doesn't know how to reject. He won't allow the hurt and the pain you have here to continue. God is Love, and Love is God: they're interchangeable. The incarnation happened for the whole of creation and not just bits of it.

"The greatest fear a human being has is not of dying but of the process of dying, dying in pain, dying alone. Part of my task is to help the person die – with dignity. Medication doesn't always stop one dying, at its best it enables us to die in the dignity of death. The tragedy with AIDS is that we can forecast what will happen. In

Britain we are about 2–3 years behind America. New York now has an equal ratio of men and women infected with the AIDS virus. There are explanations for this: there is a drug link, a prostitution link, but the point I am making here is that there is a role of compassionate empathy for the Church in it all. The Church must discover what that role is and be prepared not to count the cost. We are made strong in our weaknesses: through recognising and not being put down by them. For example, the Church should accept that it has got priests and others who are gay, who lead responsible lives, and who need the Church, as much as the Church needs them.

"Working with people who are HIV infected, who are living and dying, is a fantastic experience which has taught me so much about the humanity of spirituality. These people are so vulnerable; they've nothing else to hide and they are so truthful, so trusting. They've had to 'come out' twice, once that they're gay and then a second time that they have the virus. What I have to give is my being there with them, first as a vulnerable person, then as a priest. I offer the 'body of Christ' into their hands; I drink with them from the chalice. This is important if we are to authenticate rather than push them away; at the same time they must be allowed to reject me. But the experience of caring for these young people who are dying can be overwhelming. The funeral or cremation service is also the beginning of the healing process for those who are bereaved."

Streetwise Youth

THIS IS AN organisation, set up in 1985 by Bill Kirkpatrick and Richie McMullen with the prime purpose of empowering young men away from their prostitutional activities, and researching how and why they become involved. "Teenage male prostitution is a big worry," says Bill Kirkpatrick. "There is a good likelihood that young men who indulge in prostitutional activities will pick up the virus. Almost 100% of our client group at our day centre for Streetwise Youth are homeless. These boys are faced with using prostitution as the one tried and tested means available to them of survival. It is highly unlikely that infected young persons will reveal their condition to the men who set out to use and abuse them. Nor do the infected men declare their own condition. Thus infection spreads. We offer a day centre facility to these young men, but they also need a residential facility. For various reasons most of the boys we see have either been through or cannot cope with agencies offering emergency assistance of any kind. In addition some of these agencies feel they cannot cope with those who have been exposed to the kind of 'streetwise' survival we are discussing.

"The only weapon we've got is education; there's nothing else. I'm very worried about teenagers in general, no just those we meet through Streetwise Youth. At that age boys and girls are very sexual persons and likely to be experimenting. The urge is there and nothing will stop the urge. The challenge is to educate young folk, to adopt a responsible behaviour pattern without making them frightened of sex either. Sex must be seen as a wonderful gift to be offered and received – in a co-creative way. Above all, we have got to be realistic. If a young person has become involved in prostitutional activities, there's a reason why and we must give him time to test us and feel safe with us. Then, we might be able to empower him. It's no good our going on the street and saying 'Stop your sexual activity tonight!' It's utterly unrealistic. I have not gone into any details about young women involved in prostitutional activities for two reasons. One is that people are more aware of young girls in this scene, and secondly most of our work is with young men. Wel-care and other agencies have more experience of young girls and women caught up in this scene. No doubt the hazards are similar for all inexperienced young pesons. For many, their reasons for getting involved are similar, such as the need of the very basics in life, like food, housing, and companionship of a peer group."

Keeping going

THE MOST REMARKABLE thing to those who know Bill Kirkpatrick is that he has managed to keep going all these years. How does he do it? "Well," he says, "I pray. I started with a pattern of prayer, but more and more this has changed. I like to think that what I'm doing every day is a prayer. Each morning I have an hour of silence, on my own, in the little chapel of Saint Mary Magdalene and Saint

Barnabas, under the pavement of Warwick Road, where I also celebrate the eucharist. I pray, too, during the day when it's appropriate to do so and celebrate at other times in the week and on Sundays at Saint Cuthbert's Church, Philbeach Gardens, our local Anglican church. I also have a spiritual director, a woman; I think it's important it should be a woman given the work I do and the fact I am single. I am a priest associate of the Sisters of the Love of God at Fairacres in Oxford, go there or to one of their other houses for a few days. I'm often not in bed until the early hours. I get my sleep on my days off. I don't get disturbed too often during the night, but I'm always available whenever I'm in my flat, and there is an answerphone. Basically, I'm one of those people who needs to be terribly busy – or do nothing. My work is to enable others to recognise that God loves them. This is shown to the young person and others, as I attempt to be alongside, as a person who loves. We are together empowered to love, through the constant loving of our ultimate lover – God, the Father/Mother of us all."

Father Bill Kirkpatrick runs "Reaching Out", a listening and counselling service in Earl's Court, and has recently been appointed the full-time director of "Streetwise Youth". He is also the author of AIDS: Sharing the Pain, *a practical guide for all involved in the pastoral care of those infected with and affected by HIV infection, published by Darton, Longman and Todd, £4.95. ISBN 0 232 517487.*

On Sheep and Shepherds

Gillian and Ivan Walton

IN SOUTH LONDON facing the South Circular Road, the notice board of St Mark's Church, Battersea Rise, in addition to detailing the usual times of services, has an unusual statement: MINISTERS: THE CONGREGATION. Lest the reader should think that this is a witness to one of the more autonomous forms of Protestantism, the notice makes it clear that St Mark's is part of the Church of England and the name of the vicar is written above in equally bold letters. The form of the ministry is not detailed, particularly in what sense if at all it extends to the thousands who drive by every day on that notoriously tedious road. But, by including the congregation under the title of minister, St Mark's expresses a mood of the Church which is current and affirms the importance of lay people (or "the laity"), where such are defined as all church members who are not clergy of one kind or another. *All are Called*[1] is a recent collection of essays from a working party of the General Synod Board of Education, which emphasises the central truth that all Christians are intrinsically of equal worth and all are to live their faith in every aspect of their lives. Going to church is not a bolt-on extra to an otherwise secular life. Rather, all Christians are the Church, whose head is Christ:

> "The Church is ministry;" that is to say, the Church cannot be separated from its task, and ministry cannot be severed from what it is to be a Christian. . . . There is no such thing as the Spirit-less or gift-less Christian: each person is a "minister" in his or her own right.[2]

Much of *All are Called* is about how this truth can best be expressed in an organisation (also, confusingly, called "the Church"), which has strong structural and hierarchical elements and whose government is often perceived as remote, unrepresentative and undemocratic; and inevitably it is concerned also with the often vexed question of the relationship between lay people and the clergy.

The scope for difficulties and misunderstanding is very great and we shall illustrate this by telling a personal story. One Sunday morning we attended the service at a famous and very well-attended London church. The distinguished preacher took as his text the passage in which St Paul says farewell to the elders of Ephesus and bids them to: "Keep watch over yourselves and all the flock of which the Holy Spirit has made you overseers. Be shepherds of the Church of God."[3]

The sermon, clearly a model of its kind, engaged close attention and many members of the congregation took notes. For our theme, the main interest was the very clear demarcation made between "shepherds" and "the flock", or "sheep." Shepherds are teachers, pastors, trained and dedicated people who look after and discipline the sheep, and indeed attract new ones to the fold. There is an urgent need for more shepherds, thus defined. Sheep, on the other hand alas, are poor, feeble creatures, described from the pulpit on the good authority of a farmer known to the preacher, as stubborn, wilful and stupid. This point went down well and there was laughter. There was also a hidden agenda. Were we to deduce from what we had heard that we had discovered a congregation of five hundred shepherds? Through an overworked biblical metaphor, a pervasive hierarchy between teacher and taught, leader and led, was being unconsciously promulgated. We departed that morning and wondered: if the only role for the ordinary Christian, for the lay person, is to be a sheep, who will remain a Christian?

It is probably true that most Christians take the hierarchical aspects of their Churches with a pinch of salt, accepting that some form of organisation is necessary. Nevertheless, if part of the truth of *All are called* is that there are no first and second class citizens in the people of God, there are very serious questions about how the organised Church, particularly its governing and controlling elements, reflects the demographic composition of its members. The representation of lay people and the proportion of men to women in Church structures of government are quite simply grossly out of proportion to the actual numbers who are members of the Church of England. To belong to that organisation, for all its other virtues, is to accept a substantial degree of clerical domination as part of its very fabric. When combined with the shepherd-sheep mode of thought, the whole is a powerful formula for the perpetual infantilisation and eventual alienation of a large part of the Church. Although there are various ways in which the organisation may be adjusted to reflect and emphasise the role of lay people, the problem with creating "official" designations for them – as lay readers, group leaders and the like – is that while important in themselves, they may serve to perpetuate hierarchical models, with the lines of division shifted.

In our opinion, it is attitudes which are the foundation of structures. What does being the "people of God" really mean? How can each person be an effective "minister in his or her own right"?

We may begin an answer to these questions by describing our experience in writing this article. Initially, Ivan's approach tended to be structured and rational, whereas Gillian's was interior and intuitive. There was a phase of listening and discussion before the final article took shape, quite different we believe, than either of us could have written alone. Had we not listened, we could have come into conflict and rejected the other's view as alien, as a way of coping with our own feelings of being misunderstood. This theme of alienation is of crucial importance. For example, it is central to the story of the Fall in Genesis 3. Adam and Eve take for themselves the knowledge of Good and Evil, and as a consequence become rivals of God who created them. The story has such enduring power because it places alienation at the very heart of our human condition. All of us experience alienation – some, God knows, much more than others – from one another, from a sense of wholeness or belonging, and from God. For ourselves or through others we all experience death and bereavement, sickness of mind and body, family conflicts, our sinfulness and that of others, old age, even war, violence, and famine. These experiences create powerful feelings, sometimes too powerful to be accommodated, which we may cope with in various ways. We may deny them: that is, ignore them or pretend that they do not exist or are unimportant. In the case of unwanted or destructive emotions we may project them on to other people, which is a form of denial, and then attack in them those parts of ourselves we cannot bear. We may accept our experiences fatalistically, as inevitable. Finally, we may accept the experiences and the feelings they evoke as part of our lives, learn from them, and put them at the disposal of other people.

We would suggest that this last is the way nearest to our understanding of Christ's work and of our own witness as Christians. We take comfort from the fact that Jesus fully experienced what it is to be human. For us, his ultimate triumph over death at the hands of evil and worldly men is a hope and inspiration, to set against the universality of suffering. His healing of the sick, the raising of the dead, and the calming of the waters, are not only a demonstration of his power and his lordship, but also they point to a new Kingdom, a new order which begins in this life for those who believe in him. We see the gospel accounts as showing Jesus not shrinking or flinching from difficult situations or encounters. Instead, He meets them face to face and transforms them. Our understanding of our Faith is that at baptism we die with Christ to mere worldliness and we rise with Him to new life. We are enabled to acknowledge our faults. We are asked to trust in Christ in prayer, and to the power of the Spirit in our lives so that we too may face the situations in which we find ourselves, and reach out to others, created as we all are in the image of God.

Our understanding of ministry encompasses a commitment to love others in such a way as to offer acceptance and understanding of their areas of painful and negative feelings. If we ourselves have not had the experience of having had our own difficult, deviant and conflict-full areas accepted and managed by others, then we cannot bear them ourselves. We are frightened by them and do our best to dispose of them, often to the detriment of others. This containment of pain and fear is firstly the task for parents, but if it does not happen then, life offers chances of redemption in other relationships later. As "ministers" we have the resource of the Grace of God and we have our human selves. God's Grace is free and beyond our power to control. We can, nevertheless, prepare ourselves to be the means by which others can experience it.

Thus, how we have been helped to cope with our own alienation affects crucially how we may meet and attempt to transform the alienation of others. Our own needs for love and understanding do

not diminish as we grow older. To say that our experience of alienation may be put at the disposal of others is not to pry into their
private affairs, or to attempt to prise out personal details of their
lives which they are reluctant to divulge. Nor is it to smugly or
ostentatiously force our own experiences onto others. We are not
suggesting mawkish sentimentality or morbid curiosity. Rather, we
are describing what we believe to be a proper availability or accessi-
bility of person to person.

> We begin with persons in society in the present. What is the lay task
> there? It is the task of searching for, holding to, living, struggling, and
> dying in, the "creative centre of the culture" (to use, in a fresh context,
> a phrase of Charles Davis) to which we belong; it is here that the Word
> (John 1,1), we may believe, is to be found as the ultimate light and the
> reason of human beings. The creative centre of culture. . . . is found at
> those critical points in society where God's creativity and redemptive acts
> are contending with forces of meaninglessness, dispersion, disorder and
> despair.[4]

Availability of person to person is, we believe, a "creative centre"
for the Church. It is a living, dynamic contact of Christians with one
another and with non-Christians. The Church grows if these contacts
transform the lives of others; or it is diminished if they do not.

Except in the special circumstances of sacramental confession, this
sharing of our alienation and the healing which may follow, are not
services performed by the clergy for the laity. All may serve one
another. All have responsibilities and all have needs. Roles change
according to time and occasion. A definition of counselling from the
British Association for Counselling (1980) is relevant in this context
too:

> People become engaged in counselling when a person, occupying regularly
> or temporarily the role of counsellor offers or agrees explicitly to offer
> time, attention and respect to another person or persons temporarily in
> the role of client.

This emphatically is not a model of sheep and shepherds. It is
truer to say that all are sheep and all are shepherds. If clergy and
laity collude together to put the clergy into the position of parent
figures, the clergy then become available for unbearably strong pro-

jections from the laity, as idealisation or criticism, which can make their own personal lives untenable and lead to their finding it very difficult to distinguish between what belongs to their role and what to their person. A shift in the balance of responsibility towards the laity, a "growing up" of attitudes, will relieve the clergy of the burden; enable them to deal with the business of their own human destiny; and redistribute the projective system.

If we fail to acknowledge our alienation, we construct defences which alienate others. These defences may include our religion itself. Membership of the Church, and of roles within it, is often in danger of being used as a defence against feelings of alienation and personal anguish, which in order for us to be fully human and in the fully human image of Christ, need to be experienced. A self-defensive system substitutes Christ's holy Church with a potentially harmful and all too creaturely institution; and in this direction lie self-righteousness, self-seeking, stereotyping of others and eventual destruction.

A pervasive view has been that the centre of energy and power rests within the institution of the Church, with its bishops and clergy, its public voice and its synods, and it is this that feeds the world outside, both lay Christian and non-Christian. The Church crusades, teaches, directs and exhorts; and simultaneously in its history it has often either denigrated or idealised women. Often it has not sufficiently valued those listening, receptive, intuitive and integrative skills which may be described as feminine. Feminine is not the same as female but is often falsely identified as such, and the false view of the female tends to an understatement of feminine values. We would suggest that there is a need for a paradigm shift to a view which can recognise in the interface of men and women with all areas of life the dynamic of God's work, and that it is often the task of the lay Christian to recognise and release that dynamic wherever she or he finds her or himself. Therefore it is mostly the laity who bring this life back into the institution; it is they who revitalise it. The laity are the prophets of the Church. The prophets of old – Elijah, Elisha and Isaiah – were outside the legalistic structures, and were symbolically and actually in the wilderness. Being a Christian is not cosy. The insistent call to proclaim the Kingdom of God challenges our worldly presuppositions and priorities, yet simultaneously our engagement with the world does not allow us to occupy a permanent haven behind the fortifications of a merely institutional church.

Gillian Walton works as a marital psychotherapist. Her husband, Ivan, is a consultant physician who specialises in the medicine of elderly people.

Ordination and pastoral care

Roger Greenacre and Jeremy Haselock

IF THERE IS in this country a general sentiment of respect and sympathy for the clergy among those whose attachment to the Church is minimal or non-existent, this is largely because the ordained ministry is perceived – not without reason – as belonging to the 'caring' professions. Many have had first- or second-hand experience of receiving pastoral care in sickness, bereavement or some other form of personal crisis, of having a visit at home, in hospital or in prison, or of having turned in a crisis to a priest because he seemed the most appropriate (or only appropriate) person to turn to at a moment of need. We should be grateful for such a perception, and perhaps grateful for the established nature and parochial structure of the Church of England in that it is more often than not 'the Vicar' to whom the needy turn. We should be worried whenever or wherever the perception is absent, although it has to be recognized that it is not without its dangers. The priest can be seen simply as a counsellor for individuals with personal problems and his role can be divorced from its specifically Christian character (for Christians are not the only people to care) and from its specific foundation in the ministry of word and sacrament. While it is true to say that in the sixteenth-century English Reformation there was a new emphasis on the pastoral role of the ordained ministry, given clear and strong expression in the new rites of ordination, the English Ordinal did not abandon the word priest or the concept of priesthood. In becoming more clearly a pastor, the priest does not cease to be a priest.

What then is the relation between priest and pastor? Does the deacon have a distinctive pastorate? Where does the bishop fit in? These are important questions theologically and ecumenically; they are also important questions for the ordained minister's own self-understanding, for there can be, and often is, a tension in his life and in the exercise of his office between the 'priestly' and the 'pastoral' demands of his ministry. The *crise d'identité* experienced by many clergy in the late '50s and '60s, with the growth of sociology as an academic discipline in our universities and the consequent rise of the professional social worker, shows perhaps just how deep seated the confusion and tensions were then. But, there is a prior question which needs first to be resolved. The very word 'pastoral' denotes the authority of a shepherd; even abstracting from the priestly character of the ordained ministry, there is a difference in kind between the caring ministry of the caring professions and the caring ministry of one who cares precisely because he has received a share in the ministry of Christ the Good Shepherd. All the baptized share in the pastoral, prophetic and priestly ministry of Christ who is king and shepherd, prophet and high priest; but the ordained ministry shares in that ministry in a way that relates to the specific character of ordination and derives from the authority which it alone can bestow.

In the Prayer Book Ordinal the bishop in one of the questions addressed to those being ordained to the priesthood refers to "the people committed to your cure and charge". Again, in collating or instituting a parish priest the bishop speaks to him of "the cure of souls which is both yours and mine". The word 'cure' in this context – from the Latin *cura* – implies both authority and care: there cannot be the one without the other. If Christ himself is the Good Shepherd, it is because his care for people is not just the fruit of deep human compassion (important though that is) but flows from his own understanding of himself as the One who is sent by the Father and as the one who fulfils in himself the Old Testament role of messianic shepherd king; it flows above all from the eternal exchange of love between the three Persons of the Trinity and the love of the Creator for his creation which finds human embodiment in Jesus through his incarnation.

Just as there is, of course, a diversity of gifts at the service of the Church so there is a diversity of ministries springing from the same outpouring of the Holy Spirit. In order to explore the distinctive task of the ordained ministry for the people of God and answer some of the questions posed above, we need to examine each order of the historic threefold ministry in turn and assess its specific contribution to the life of the whole.

The deacon

IF THERE IS any one part of the historic threefold ministry of the Church which has a specially authentic claim to belong to the caring professions it is the order of deacons. The traditional establishment of the order, related in Acts 6.1–6, was a response to the need to set apart men to "serve tables"; in other words to exercise a practical caring ministry in the growing Christian community. Where they are mentioned by name, *diakonoi,* in the New Testament, in 1 Timothy 3.8–13 for example, it is required of them that they are honest, of good repute and gifted with the sound management of affairs so that they may deserve the trust of the community they serve. St Ignatius of Antioch, for whom his deacons were his "special favourites" and "fellow slaves", explained in his letter to the Trallians that the deacons' service to the local church clearly gives them the privileged role of visibly representing the One who came to serve the needs of all. For him too, they had to be above reproach:

> Deacons must give complete satisfaction to everyone, for they do not serve mere food and drink, but minister to God's Church. They must therefore avoid leaving themselves open to criticism, as they would shun fire.[1]

Diaconal ministry rapidly came to include a distinctive liturgical function. Service at the tables of the needy was combined with service at the table of the Lord and so in the writings of Tertullian those who are called to the order of deacon are called *ad altaris ministerium.* At the eucharist and in the daily office the deacons read the scriptural lessons and led the intercessions. Here again, in this particular, the deacons' special concern for the poor and needy members of the community made them the logical ministers to bid prayers for them. The liturgical ministry of deacons was the seal they placed on their duties and somehow a sign or symbol of their practical community service.

The scanty New Testament data and the more abundant testimony of the Patristic period are evidence of a distinctive, multi-faceted ministry; the fruitful union of particular service within the liturgical assembly and charitable action outside it. This tradition was lost in the west when the diaconate came to be viewed transitionally, as merely a stage in the process of priestly formation. Ecumenical convergence on the nature of ministry, however, has grown out of common study of the early tradition and texts such as that of Lima, *Baptism, Eucharist and Ministry,* for example, have as a result highlighted the cross fertilization of liturgical and charitable ministry in the work of the deacon:

> Deacons represent to the Church its calling as servant in the world. By struggling in Christ's name with the myriad needs of societies and persons, deacons exemplify the interdependence of worship and service in the Church's life.[2]

The recovery of the tradition has restored to the Church – if she chooses to take advantage of it – the ministry of a distinctive order of deacons and led to the reformulation of a theology of the diaconate which is both important and significant for the whole Church. For just as there is a priesthood of all the faithful into which all are admitted through baptism (1 Peter 2.5,9) so also there is a diaconate of all the faithful. Just as all Christians participate in the priesthood of Christ through incorporation into his body the Church, so too they must participate in his ministry of service (John 13.12–17). The ordained deacon engaged in diaconal ministry is a sign to the whole serving Church of the essential character of Christ's own ministry on earth. Jesus the deacon washed the feet of his disciples and purified the precincts of the Temple; he fed those who were physically hungry and rebuked those who lacked spiritual hunger. Inspired by this example, the deacon's ministry focuses the ministry of service of the whole Church, which is the response to God's call to serve the world in the name of Christ. It need hardly be pointed out that, until the Church of England takes more seriously the opening of the permanent diaconate to men as well as to women, that valuable ministry will continue to be undervalued. The signal that such a lack of affirmation sends out is that the diaconate remains a transitional ministry for men on the way to priesthood and a permanent vocation only for women.

The priest

THE SECOND ORDER of the historic threefold ministry, what the new Roman ordination rite describes as "priesthood in the presbyteral order", is in present-day Catholic tradition closely associated with the eucharist, the celebration of which is seen as the highest and most characteristic privilege of that order. Although it is clear to those with some understanding of the Church's history that, in the earlier centuries, it was the bishop who was the normal president of the eucharistic assembly and to whom strictly sacerdotal language was therefore applied, this perception is in no way erroneous. We can affirm this close link provided we get the overall context and the balance right. The controlling concept which gives meaning to the priesthood is the service of the gospel: a service which includes teaching, preaching, healing, counselling, consoling, reconciling, building up and feeding.

In the *Final Report* of ARCIC I, the key theme running through all the statements is identified as *koinonia* or 'communion'. So, the authority given to the ordained ministry exists only to serve *koinonia* and this service is expressed most fully in the presidency of the eucharistic celebration:

> The ordained minister presiding at the eucharist is a sign of Christ gathering his people and giving them his body and blood. The gospel he preaches is the gospel of unity. Through the ministry of word and sacrament the Holy Spirit is given for the building up of the body of Christ.[3]

In his presidency of the eucharist therefore, the priest is not only exercising his specifically priestly task of representing Christ as our great high priest, he is also acting as pastor gathering his flock together and feeding them, and as herald of the gospel, proclaiming and interpreting the good news of Christ. He is leading the Church's worship, offering with God's people spiritual sacrifice[4] on behalf of all mankind, interceding for the Church and for the world; he is also speaking to mankind in the name of Christ and with his authority, offering, explaining and applying to them the Gospel of reconciliation and *koinonia,* leading the whole priestly people of God in their ministry of witness, service and care to and for the rest of mankind. So it is that *The Household of God* can say of the priest:

> When he presides at the eucharist in which all Christians, intimately united with the crucified and risen Lord and with one another, are offered anew to God, he is most clearly seen as an agent of Christ, of the Church, and of the bishop, and he represents for the eucharistic assembly the unity of Christ in all his people.[5]

His own caring ministry is set within this two way traffic of facing God on behalf of mankind and facing mankind on behalf of God; it is in this sense an extension of his liturgical ministry. It is an extension of his own liturgical ministry in another sense too; much of his caring ministry is a direct consequence of his work of baptizing, absolving, anointing, joining in marriage, blessing and burying. As we learn from *The Final Report:*

> Within the whole history of mankind the Church is to be the community of reconciliation. All ministries are used by the Holy Spirit for the building up of the Church to be this reconciling community for the glory of God and the salvation of man . . . . The goal of the ordained ministry is to serve this priesthood of all the faithful.[6]

The bishop

A CONVENIENT starting point for our theological reflection on the specific contribution of episcopal ministry to the caring ministry of the Church is provided in the Mission and Ministry section of the Lambeth Conference Report of 1988 which includes an outline of certain elements which are to be regarded as crucial in the exercise of episcopal ministry. The bishop is:

(a) a symbol of the unity of the Church in its mission;
(b) a teacher and defender of the Faith;
(c) a pastor of the pastors and of the laity;

(d) an enabler in the preaching of the word, and in the administration of the sacraments;

(e) a leader in mission and an initiator of outreach to the world surrounding the community of the faithful;

(f) a shepherd who nurtures and cares for the flock of God;

(g) a physician to whom are brought the wounds of society;

(h) a voice of conscience within the society in which the local Church is placed;

(i) a prophet who proclaims the justice of God in the context of the Gospel of loving redemption;

(j) a head of the family in its wholeness, its misery and its joy. The bishop is the family's centre of life and love.[7]

It is not possible for us to comment on all these elements but it may be useful to underline some of them.

Referring back to ARCIC I's theme of the service of *koinonia* it should be noted at once that the bishop is a symbol of unity or, more positively perhaps, an agent of unity, continuity and communion in the Church, representing the universal Church to the particular local Church he leads, and representing the local to the universal. His particular care must be for the avoidance of dissension and division, for the promotion of reconciliation and unity, and so his teaching role cannot be divorced from his role of maintaining or restoring unity.

The bishop is the personal embodiment of the pastoral ministry of oversight, a ministry calling for patience, vigilance, compassion, love and authority. He it is who carries the shepherd's staff and embodies the Good Shepherd's loving leadership of the flock. He is supremely *pastor pastorum,* a pastor to his pastors, and it is worth noting that it is precisely this aspect of his ministry which is leading many in the non-episcopal Churches to appreciate the need to give personal embodiment to *episkope.* He is also pastor and father in God to all his people, although not in a way that interferes or clashes with the relationship of his priests with the people committed to their care.

The bishop is the primary minister of word and sacrament. His *cathedra* is not so much the throne of a ruler as the chair from which he teaches and from which he presides over the eucharist. No eucharist is fully the Church's eucharist unless it is celebrated in communion with the bishop and as a participation in his eucharist.

The 'naming' of the diocesan bishop at every mass should therefore be a liturgical imperative. His role in Christian initiation through confirmation should underline the role of the bishop in the process whereby Christians grow into full and active membership of the body of Christ.

The bishop is a leader in mission; he has to be the father not of an inward looking group but of all under his jurisdiction, a man sensitive to the particular needs and opportunities facing the human family resident in his diocese and capable of exercising apostolic and prophetic leadership within the Church in tackling these needs and opportunities. The authority reserved to the bishop to continue the orderly transmission of the ordained ministry in the sacrament of holy order witnesses to his responsibility for the continuing mission of the Church and its service of the Gospel.

The bishop is, to quote the Prayer Book Ordinal, a "father in God" and in the classic liturgical tradition of the Church his order alone is thus addressed. If today priests can also be addressed and referred to as 'Father', it is only because they have a share by extension in the ministry of the bishop as head of a family. There is something specifically paternal in the loving and caring responsibility which the bishop has for his people.

All this is concisely summed up in *The Household of God:*

> The bishop has responsibility to teach the Faith, to encourage, promote and maintain the proclamation in word and deed of the apostolic gospel and to care for that flock of Christ, clergy and people alike, committed to his charge. The bishop has the fullness of ministry and has in himself all other ministries. Within the local Church, the diocese over which he has jurisdiction, he is the representative of the universal Church and the fount of its sacramental, evangelical and pastoral life. Constantly supported by the prayers of his clergy and people, he is to be respected and obeyed as he watches over and prays for those committed to his charge, and teaches and governs them after the example of the apostles, speaking in the name of God and interpreting to them the gospel of Christ.[8]

As we have already tried to show, to ascribe to the sacerdotal ministry of bishop and priest a specific quality of priestliness in no way derogates from the priestly character and responsibility of the whole people of God and to ascribe to all three orders of the historic ministry a specific pastoral quality in no way derogates from the pastoral character and responsibility of the whole people of God. Lay people must not consider themselves as simply being on the receiving end of the pastoral ministrations of the clergy but also and above all as being active partners with the clergy in the Church's mission and service to the world. A final quotation from *The Household of God* may serve to make this clearer:

> All baptized members are called to represent Christ and his Church, to bear witness to him wherever they may be, and to bring hope in places of darkness and despair. According to their gifts, they continue, in the face of division and conflict, Christ's reconciling work.[9]

Roger Greenacre is Canon Chancellor of Chichester Cathedral, a member of the General Synod of the Church of England and of the Anglican – Roman Catholic Committee in England, and has spent 10 years of his ministry in France. Jeremy Haselock is Domestic Chaplain to the Bishop of Chichester and previously served assistant curacies in London in Pimlico and Paddington. They are co-authors of a recently-published study of the Holy Week liturgy, The Sacrament of Easter, *a substantial revision of a work originally published in 1965 as a direct result of a course of Lent sermons given at St Mary's, Bourne Street, in 1963.*

Lost Sheep

John Gilling

IF ALL THE PEOPLE who have been baptised in England decided to go
to church one Sunday, every church in the kingdom would be hope-
lessly overcrowded: even if those who were confirmed or had become
full communicant members of their various denominations were to
do likewise, there would hardly be room for them. Yet, in fact, even
for the principal services at Easter and Christmas, let alone the main
services Sunday by Sunday, many of our churches are more than
half empty. This is true not only in rural areas, where vast churches
are built for a population larger and more observant in past centuries,
but also in our great cities, where the enthusiasm of Victorian church
builders has bequeathed us an embarrassing and expensive richness
of Gothic near-masterpieces, some of them falling into ruin as too
costly to maintain and too highly listed to destroy. What the statistics
of the present century seem to show is a gradual decline in the use
of the church for the traditional rites of passage of the Christian
community: baptisms, confirmations, marriages and funerals. In
addition there is, as no doubt there always has been, a sharp decline,
a heavy wastage; only a small proportion of those incorporated into
Christ by their baptism remain active members of the Church. The
phrase 'the sleeping church', originally coined to describe the rest of
the holy souls of Christians after death, could nowadays be used of
the majority of the baptised in this land. We are left with an active
church membership of less than 10 per cent of the population.

This situation, although it may vary considerably from country to
country, is characteristic of all the countries of western Europe, the
exception being Ireland where (as in Poland) the life of the nation
is still deeply steeped in religious loyalty and to be a Catholic or a
Protestant defines one's life and one's hopes. And, looking to East-

69

ern Europe, where there is felt to be oppression and injustice, the Church has often become an effective focus of protest as has also happened in Latin America with its theology of Christ as liberator. In the Americas, as in Africa, the relevance of Christianity to the political and economic problems of life has resulted in a growing, developing church, though some of its manifestations appear to European eyes uncongenial and dangerous.

It is thus not everywhere that the tide of faith is on the ebb: nor is it on the flood only in the developing countries, for in the last decade the influence of committed believers has certainly made itself felt against the eastern agnostic establishment in the United States, even if some of the evangelists have proved to have betrayed the morality of the majority. If we look outward, south and east and west, we can at least realise that the position in our own country is not a result of some inevitable historical development by which the secular must triumph over the spiritual. Moreover, even in England, the decline in religious observance is by no means universal; the evangelical movement, influenced by the revival of charismatic elements, grows within and across the denominational divides in house groups and churches; the Roman Catholic Church holds its own, while Orthodoxy wins new recruits. The falling off is most noticeable, firstly among many of the traditional Protestant churches and secondly in the Established Church.

Churchgoing is not, of course, an absolutely certain indicator of the vitality of faith in the community. Any pastor or member of a mission team comes to know while visiting that from time to time one comes across households steeped in prayer and in Christian moral conviction but with little or no relationship with any organised church, though I suspect these are less common than in the past. The discipline imposed by the different Christian bodies varies enormously both in principle and in practice; for Roman Catholics not to be at mass on Sundays and days of obligation is a serious sin; for Anglicans even the rule of receiving holy communion three times a year has become a dead letter. So the statistics of decline need to be treated with some caution as an indicator of what is happening to Christianity in England: many would still think of themselves as Christians and as members of the Church of England, though they rarely attend its services; Roman Catholics, who by the rules of their

Church have lapsed, know they are bad Catholics but still have a residual loyalty to the faith of their fathers. All this goes some way to explain why, in answer to various questionnaires, a large majority of those who respond declare that they believe in God, even if the rest of their answers show that their beliefs are by no means necessarily orthodox or in accordance with traditional Christianity. It seems that the situation in England is rather similar to that in Greece where the vast majority of citizens say they are members of the Orthodox Church but this seems to have little effect either in attendance at the liturgy or on public or private morality.

This survival of what is often called folk religion has its importance politically and commercially; we like a certain religious flavour in the life of the state; royal and national occasions are marked by church celebrations such as on Remembrance Sunday and *par excellence* at the coronation of the monarch. Although the commercial and social significance of Christmas now far outweighs any residual religious meaning, the carols and the midnight mass give an attractive glow of religious sentiment to the eating, drinking and shopping. But, it is difficult to judge how important this icing on the Xmas cake is in the life of the nation: it may be only a feeling of nostalgia for what we once believed, for an age of faith now past as we have grown up; it may simply be evidence that we live in a post-Christian society.

The best indication of whether faith is alive or dead is the vitality of prayer in the life of the individual and this is something only God can truly see, although we can certainly make an informed guess at the state of our own spiritual lives by simply asking ourselves whether we still listen and talk to him. When I was 14 I was sent away to school: each night in my dormitory it was taken for granted that we would all kneel by our beds and say our prayers and so we did. I do not know whether this admirable habit of 50 years ago still persists. But, some 15 years ago I was made chaplain to a girls' day public school (like my own school, a church foundation) and asked the first batch of confirmation candidates whether they went to church each Sunday: none of them did and this did not surprise me. I then asked if any of them said their prayers each day: none of them did and this did surprise me. It would be very dangerous to generalise from this anecdote but I wonder . . . . And, year by year, I notice that after confirmation the girls become increasingly less regular at the school eucharist. It is almost as if confirmation acted as some kind of inoculation against the practice of the faith.

Of course, there are many pressures which act against Christianity in our society. Of these probably the least significant is deliberate atheist propaganda: I suspect that reading an attack on religion makes us often react in its favour. Indeed, atheism seems to have been largely ineffective even in countries where it has been industriously propagated by the state for a generation or more. Perhaps more influential and pervasive have been the deeply thought philosophical or historical television series which have subjected Christianity to the acid of rationalism: we may count it fortunate that, however high the quality of such programmes may be, they attract only a small minority of viewers. Even more widespread is the cumulative marginalising of the spiritual dimension of life in all the popular forms of entertainment: the television and radio networks and the serious press maintain religious correspondents and advisers but there is not much to remind us in the soaps and in *The Sun* of fundamental issues of life and faith. And the way we live now, getting and spending, is too much filled with business and leisure activities to give us the space seriously to think and so to balance our minds against the unthinking materialism which we absorb as we sit passively before our television screens and videos. The fact is that, when we meet other people, the natural topics of conversation are the weather and our everyday concerns; the last thing we consider is anything to do with religion, not because, as in the past, it is too controversial but simply because we do not think of it.

We English identify the real world with the material world: "Distracted from distraction by distraction"[1] we forget the world of value, of beauty, truth and goodness. And we are encouraged in this by humanity's apparent control of its own destiny through applied science and social engineering: we are brought to consider as of right the benefits of a welfare state and the rule of law. In fact we know that the comparative affluence of our lives is bought at a dangerous price in the exploitation of natural resources, at the expense of the pollution of the environment and the impoverishment of the developing countries: we go on still, hoping that the day of reckoning may be put off by further developments in man's knowledge and control and that Utopia will come. The global quality of the problems lead us to a certain irresponsibility: "they will have to see to it", an irresponsibility already encouraged in us by the idea that we are entitled to be successful in the quest for life, liberty and the pursuit of happiness. Only the illness and death of someone close to us or the tragedy of some large-scale disaster can shake us out of our complacency.

Yet, in our present situation, not everything conspires to take the part of the devil in concealing the mystery at the heart of things. Over the last 50 years, though, alas, at the cost of immense human suffering, we have seen the collapse of societies built on the basis of human omnicompetence. The first to fall were the fascist and national socialist empires; now it seems that what was known as dialectical materialism, scientific socialism or simply communism, the doctrine which controlled the policies of the nations of a great part of the world, is crumbling as a result of its own inadequacy in fulfilling its prophecies. The age of faith in atheism which dominated half our century may now be reaching its end. The alternatives to the religious view of life are largely discredited: the danger being that seven other devils may come to fill the credal vacuum, the hope being that it may be faith in Christ.

The first priority in this situation is for the Church to care for the flock, the faithful few, the 10 per cent who are still practising Christians, but we have our Lord's own authority in believing that this care must also include seeking the lost sheep, those already by baptism members of the flock, those who have been made members of the body of Christ but who have strayed from the way. It is true that for many of those their Christian education may have been limited to an occasional attendance at a Sunday school, such participation in worship as school assemblies may have given, possibly instruction before confirmation and very irregular visits to their parish church, together with what they may have absorbed from the religious slots on radio or television.

The time is ripe, if the Christian community in the parish is ready, for a revival of something like the traditional mission, a lively celebration of the faith, with teaching on prayer and doctrine. The chief problem lies usually within the body of practising Christians in the Church: in Anglican parishes, even in those with comparatively large congregations, there is a tendency to evade the call to evangelism, a complacency which ignores the outsider; there is also a traditional English delicacy about butting in and interfering with other people. This makes a general visitation of the parish very difficult for the visitors as well as for those who are visited, so it is essential that as much as possible is done to prepare the teams or groups of those visiting house by house before they begin their task. It takes at least two years of preparation before such a mission can take place. Great care has to be taken over the style as well as the content of what is to be said: it should take account of the prevailing culture (difficult in so plural a society) without distorting the gospel. These problems will be reinforced by what is also inevitable in human affairs, the fact that things, however well-planned, always go wrong.

Nevertheless, no national mission by some great star missioner, nor what is to come by way of religious propaganda over our televisions in the future free-for-all, can possibly replace the work of the local Christian community in the conversion and care of souls. It is true that the main result may well be the deepening of faith within the community: the effect on those outside may be transitory; but at least they have been brought into contact on their doorsteps if not in the local church itself with the fact there are Christians still alive and kicking, to whom Christ is a living reality. And some of the encounters may bear fruit. At one door in Belgravia a member of a visiting team from the local parish called with details of the coming mission. "I don't believe in God," was the strong response. "My dear, I am *so* sorry." And, within the congregation, ties of devotion to God and to each other can grow and develop into lively Christian groups, questioning their prejudices and engaged more deeply in good works. To speak personally, I was taken aback when, after a mission in my own parish, one of the groups that emerged was of young men with a call to ordination: this was, as they were of very high quality, rather a blow to the life of the parish but undoubtedly a benefit to the life of the Church at large. It is worth taking the risk of the venture. We are not simply doing something in order not to be seen doing nothing.

A mission is a sign, a metaphor, an icon of what the life of the Christian community must be. In *Religio Medici* Sir Thomas Browne talks of the nature of love and friendship:

Now, if we can bring our affections to look beyond the body, and cast an eye upon the soul, we have found out the true object not only of friendship but Charity; and the greatest happiness we can bequeath the soul, is that wherein we all do place our last felicity, Salvation; which though it be not in our power to bestow, it is in our charity and pious invocations to desire, if not to procure and further.[2]

As Christians we wish, indeed, we are bound to wish for the good of our neighbour and to do what we can to procure and further it, as we are also bound to believe that his final good (apart from any material benefit we can bestow on him) is participation in the fellowship of heaven. Catholic Christians believe that the sure way our Lord bestows the gift of the Holy Spirit and our growth in his grace is as members of his Church on earth in the sacramental life – "prayer, observance, discipline, thought and action"[3] – which delivers us from evil and begins the work of redemption in and through us.

Even though our own Christian community in our own parish may be too weak at present to undertake a mission in our own area: even though the great majority of our people are indifferent or hostile to the Church as an institution irrelevant to their immediate needs and concerns, these considerations are in no way sufficient to absolve us from our responsibility as individuals or as the Church to love our neighbour into the Faith to the best of our ability. To prepare ourselves for this task we need all the help we can get from God through the Church and through the life of prayer. He must be real in our lives before others can see him as real through us. Every Christian comes to know our Lord through other Christians: only if we ourselves enter into the redemptive life of Jesus, the paschal mystery, can we bring others into his presence. Most of us can remember, if not an actual conversion experience, moments in our lives when God has disclosed something of his reality to us. One such moment in my own life was when I was preparing for a seminar under Dom David Knowles for the History Tripos at Cambridge: he had set us the study of the ontology of Thomas Aquinas. This first gave me some idea of the glory and transcendence of God. I will always be grateful to St Thomas and to Dom David as soul friends indeed.

As far as I know neither of them has ever had any idea of their importance in my life. This may also be true of any influence we may have in bringing souls closer to God. All we can do is be honest and open with others as to our faith and what we understand of it. God does not ask of us that we should all become professional evangelists and we should not be alarmed if we feel we are such inadequate Christians that we may actually put people off even within the circle of those with whom we work and live. Most of us must have prayed for the gift of faith for those dearest to us and there seems to have been no answer to our prayer: any priest or Christian teacher is aware of those whom he has instructed and who have rejected Christianity and all its works as a deception. Those disappointments should not stop us praying or working for Christ in his lost sheep. It may be, as Julian of Norwich says in the mysterious parable in the *Revelations of Divine Love*, that there is a calling to leave God to return in the end like the prodigal son to find him again dearer than ever.

I have said nothing here about the techniques of 'church growth' or the organisation of the local community of Christians. This is due to sheer ignorance as well as lack of space to deal with these important subjects. Nor have I said anything very specific about the difficulties of working within the framework given to us by the tradition of the Churches of which we are members. As an Anglican I am constantly aware of the penalties of being in the established church, which is like walking in treacle while fighting an eiderdown. There is also added the controversy over women's ordination, which is bound to end in tears whichever side prevails and meanwhile distracts many of us and divides us from each other. But, I am afraid that all ecclesiastical organisations, like any other institutions, have their drawbacks. Fortunately they usually have their advantages too.

The greatest of these is the liturgical life of the Church. This is immensely varied and there is certainly no uniformity in worship within the various denominations, let alone between them. Yet, the effect of the liturgical movement over the last half-century and especially since the reforms of Vatican II, has been the renewal of the eucharist as the type and norm of Christian worship: even the rites authorised by the various Churches are much closer to each other, as is the theology which underlies them. It is as if the unity for which Jesus prayed on the night he was betrayed is at last gradually re-emerging in the worship of the Church: the Roman Catholic mass, the Anglican communion service, the Methodist eucharist look and feel much the same. Even the most traditional churches, which preserve the music and many of the forms dear to many of us, recognise the truth in the theology of such men as Louis Bouyer. We all recognise that the eucharist is the centre of the Christian life not just for each of us as an individual but for each congregation and for the whole Church. It is in entering the eucharistic community again that the lost sheep returns to the one fold. So, it is vital to the life of the community that however it is done it must be done as well as we can do it. It must be a celebration and not a dirge for a dead Church.

When the ambassadors of Prince Vladimir of Kiev were sent to find the true religion they came to the great church of Byzantium: of the liturgy of the eucharist they said: "Truly we did not know whether we were in this world or the next. This we know. Here God dwells among men."

John Gilling is Parish Priest of St Mary's, Bourne Street.

Christianity in the home

Judy Perkins

A TEACHER of religious studies remarked to me recently, "We say that nurture is the job of the faith communities, not of the schools; but where do you start?". We need to start just there, I think, with the 'faith community' gathered to celebrate the eucharist on Sunday. The unanimity of the parents on the priority of Sunday eucharist is an extremely important factor in the nurture of their child. Any division will lead to division in the mind of the child, and may ultimately be harmful. In passing, it may be a suitable point to question the practice of separating parents and children in church. Once it has been decided that any part of the liturgy is inappropriate for children, where is the logic in including them in another?

For many couples public liturgy is the major part of prayer in common, and domestic liturgy does not exist. Perhaps we should make more effort to cultivate it. I always feel rather envious of the domestic celebrations of Judaism especially Sabbath and Passover. I have adopted the idea of a festival table (actually the top of a chest of drawers) decorated suitably and variously throughout the year, as a focus for storytelling and celebration. But, I do have reservations about it. First, it seems more like a church celebration than a genuine domestic ritual, which I am sure should centre on food, not an 'altar'. Secondly, it seems an artificial imposition on the tradition, which has lost whatever domestic rituals it may have once had.

In many families prayer at home is essentially private. This is entirely appropriate, as in most cases members of the family are at different stages of development. One place where everyone can meet, however, is in prayer at meals. Even a brief grace is prayer in common, with which everyone can be comfortable.

With young children prayers may be said together. This is real prayer for both the parent and the child. The parent will often be the mother, both for practical reasons and more importantly because of the strength of her relationship with the child. The physical closeness between mother and child, both before and after birth gives them a bond which does not usually exist between the father and the child. This may make prayer with the mother easier for the child than prayer with the father. My own experience has been that in motherhood I have found a sense of priesthood. It is expressed when I bless my child, invoking for him the support of the hosts of heaven, and in blessing the food which symbolizes and summarizes my care for my family.

Children can learn the 'standard' prayers – the Sign of the Cross the Lord's Prayer, Hail Mary, Glory be, the Creed – and gradually contribute prayers of 'thank you' and 'sorry' and simple intercessions. Once children have outgrown prayer with their parents they can still have a corner or wall of their bedrooms as a focus for prayer, with a crucifix, icon, or pictures. At this stage the 'festival table' may still be useful for occasional celebrations for the whole family.

Bringing up a child in faith must include the transmission of the story. It is important that as children grow older they should become aware of the critical study of Scripture so that their understanding develops in accordance with their age. Children who never progress from children's Bible stories may eventually discard them with Father Christmas and the tooth fairy.

One of the hardest facts for parents to accept is that the outcome of their efforts is beyond their control. It seems that no matter how careful parents are some children will lapse while others find faith after a very different upbringing. Despite this, parents must take a long view. They are trying to give their child not just a good start but a faith that will survive their teenage years into jobs and marriage, and be passed in turn to their own children. This brings us back to the central role of the Sunday eucharist as the nexus that will carry a child into adulthood.

Judy Perkins is a wife and mother and head of religious studies at the Lady Eleanor Holles School, Hampton, Middlesex.

Education in the parish and beyond

John Cullen

I The buck stops here!

ONE OF THE fundamenal elements in being a Christian is the sharing of stories. Principally this sharing of stories is the process of handing on the Christian story, but by 'the Christian story' I mean not just the narratives of God's dealing with his people as related in the Old and New Testaments of our Bible, I mean also the whole faith tradition of God's pilgrim peoples throughout history as expressed in worship, statements of belief, organisational structures, forms of ministry and the lives of individuals who have been inspired and transformed by the tradition.[1]

But, the 'handing on' of the story is only *part* (albeit the principal part) of the sharing enterprise, for the Christian story is an on going one and is to be taken up, engaged, wrestled with and related to the individual stories of women, men and children of every age. This means a process of encounter between our individual stories and the community's story, allowing us, in the light of our own stories, to question and affirm the community's story, and equally, exposing ourselves to be affirmed and encouraged but also questioned and challenged by the community's story.

For the majority of practising Christians the most natural focus for this enterprise of sharing of stories will be the parish community. Within their parishes they have the opportunity of hearing the Christian story recounted, experiencing the story being celebrated, and seeing the story lived out in the lives of others. But, the most urgent and disturbing question that is being asked of parishes today is: while there may be many opportunities within parish life for people to hear or experience the community's story, what opportunities are there for people to share their own stories with one another, to see their stories in the light of the community's story, that broader story of the whole faith tradition, that story of how people have responded and failed to respond to God's actions and invitations throughout history?

The most readily available opportunities for people to experience Christian nurture are within the context of public worship which – no matter how lively, awe inspiring or imaginative – is bound by very definite constraints. Within these constraints the most that can realistically be expected is that the participants will have the opportunity of hearing the community's story read, sung, expounded or even acted or danced, but then be left to apply the story to their own stories at some later time, if at all. It is this situation which John Hull, in his recent book *What Prevents Christian Adults from Learning?* describes as a 'spirituality of passivity'.[2] In this pattern, which is so characteristic of adult Christian experience, one is preached at, instructed, given communion, helped, led in prayer, refreshed. But it is all a far cry from the language normally applied to a responsible adult who "enquires, studies, asks questions, discusses a point, looks things up, changes one's mind, forms a hypothesis, reaches a conclusion".[3] Such an apparent contradiction leads Hull to the discomforting conclusion:

> The spirituality of activity which is characteristic of children's life within the Churches does not lead naturally into the spirituality of passivity which is so often characteristic of adult life. It is not surprising that so many young people have to find their adulthood outside the Churches.[4]

If however we believe that one of the fundamental elements in being a Christian is the *sharing* of stories, what strategies do we need to develop at the parish level to foster such sharing and to encourage Christian adults to exercise that same degree of responsibility and activity in their life within the Christian community as they do in other facets of their lives? These were indeed the concerns which motivated the working parties which produced the report *All are Called* and the subsequent document *Called to be Adult Disciples* in which the issues already noted in this chapter are examined, specific obstacles are identified, and ways are explored by which: "The Church can discern and develop the abundant gifts and riches which the Spirit has given to the whole people of God."[5]

But, before we set out to consider issues, obstacles and strategies, there is a prior question which must be addressed. This question is: how realistic is it to place expectations or demands upon present parish structures in which many clergy feel stretched beyond all reasonable limits in trying to be 'Jacks (and Jills) of all trades', and in which lay leaders feel frustrated and disempowered because so much more is being required of them than they can possibly fulfil? This question lifts the lid on a number of 'hidden agendas' which lie beyond some of the burdensome and unreasonable demands which the personnel, both clergy and lay, at the centre of parish life have laid upon them by both Church 'authorities' further up the line and by people from within and sometimes beyond their parish community.

Despite much talk of decline in Church membership and parish statistics and the marginalising of parochial life in the interests of those who would still wish to be counted in the parish roll, people within and outside the parish community still look to 'their parish' as a focus or resource to meet a whole assortment of human needs. There are the expectations that within the life of any or every parish there should be resources to help individuals answer questions and cope with a whole range of situations which arise because of deficiencies in home life, in the work place, in the life of the wider community and even in life at the national level. All these areas of need are of course real and the requests which come from them legitimated but how can any or every parish community realistically be expected to have resources to hand to deal with issues of such complexity as in the list just mentioned: domestic life, employment (or unemployment), social networks, and national politics? And yet we are constantly being reminded that Christian faith is concerned with and involved in all areas of life, personal and corporate, or it is concerned with none at all.

II Reassessing priorities and resources

THE ONLY WAY in which a beleaguered parish leadership can come to terms with this impossible situation is to be fiercely realistic with itself and with those for whom it is responsible. This first and obvious strategy may mean coming to terms with some unpalatable truths and admitting that some areas of need, no matter how legitimate or pressing in themselves, are just not able to be dealt with under present circumstances and with resources currently available. It is surely better to concentrate energies in those areas which can be managed adequately rather than dissipate energy over a much wider area only to contribute to a sense of frustration and failure when it is recognized that certain tasks are being done inadequately or so ineffectively that they would be better not tackled at all. It takes considerable courage and not a little humility to propose an apparent reduction of parish activities or services, particularly if the parish has been known in the recent past for the variety of activities and opportunities for service that it offered. If a task cannot be done adequately is it not doing a service to all concerned to refer requests to another agency where they can be met and managed satisfactorily?

To talk of realistic reassessment however does not always mean that one is led to reduce or withdraw services or activities. It can also invite a re-ordering of priorities and a more effective redeployment of ability and expertise which may in turn lead eventually to an extension or increase in some areas of activity. Here a very useful resource to facilitate such a local reassessment is the form of analysis and planning for action set out in 'An Audit for the Local Church' which forms Appendix A of the report *Faith in the City* produced in 1985 by the Archbishop of Canterbury's Commission on Urban Priority Areas.[6] The areas for analysis and planning suggested in this audit process have an applicability and relevance which extends far beyond the Urban Priority Areas for which it was originally written.

The questions and areas of concern raised in this analysis invite a reconsideration of the local parish, any local parish, to see itself not so much as an alternative to and substitute for life in the world, a shelter for refugees from future stock, or a bastion of moral values set over agains a 'naughty' world outside, but rather as a vital cell and focus of energy, *divine* energy, within a wider network of cells.

In this understanding of itself the Church can begin to see itself realistically, unencumbered by past delusions of grandeur or self importance, and liberated to offer its experience and expertise in those areas more directly related to its role as an agent in the bringing in of God's Kingdom. Thus the parish can come to find itself feeding into, but also, where appropriate, being fed from, the wider community within which it is set.

For some this modification of the local Church's role within the wider community, involving a new model of engagement and collaboration with 'secular' agencies and services, may appear threatening, and a diminution of the traditional understanding of the Church's function and status. But if the notion of servant, which was embraced and embodied by our Lord himself, means anything at all, it means engagement with, and at least on equal terms with, those among whom it seeks to offer its service in the name of the servant Lord. No other agency within society is potentially as well equipped as the Church to be an agent of nurture, inspiration, reconciliation, pastoral care, enrichment, and healing – for all these services are committed to us by the Lord of the Church, and are elements in the process of salvation which it is our responsibility to promote.

III Building in love

THIS IMAGE of the Church working as servant, offering its particular gifts and insights in collaboration with other agencies and resources, is very much in line with the text which forms the theme for this book. The metaphor which is presented in Ephesians 4 is one of growth and development rather than one of construction with building materials. The full text of verse 16 speaks of the whole body being bonded and knit together by every constituent joint and, "when each part is working properly" (RSV), making bodily growth and upbuilding itself in love. This organic metaphor is much closer to our understanding of mutual enrichment by sharing of stories, resources, and experience than a structural model, and furthermore it accords with current thinking about the specific task of education.

For too long the Church has understood education, and particularly religious education, as a didactic exercise, imparting information to the ignorant. Since the pioneering work of the Brazilian educationalist Paulo Freire[7], followed up by the Americans James Fowler[8] and Thomas Groome[9], and in this country Michael Jacobs[10], Anton Baumohl[11], and the contribution of Peter Ball[12], and others working in catechumenate development, the emphasis in adult religious education has become concerned with the religious thinking and behaviour of adults and not merely with their knowledge and understanding of religion. The major influence in bringing about this shift in emphasis has been the work of Freire, particularly his techniques for raising a critical consciousness, and the concept of the three-fold process of experience (reflecting on who and where we are) – reflection (consideration of the goals that our faith sets before us) – action (developing a strategy of the ways and means of proceeding from where we are to those goals), now claimed to be the dominant process in adult religious education.[13]

The adoption of this three-fold process has had significant and revolutionary consequences for adult religious education, acknowledging the fact that the goal of the educational process is to enable people to change their situation and so modify their experience[14]. Further consequences of this change are: respect for the validity of the learners' own experience as a starting point in the educative process, and secondly, the recognition that the experience of all of us, teacher and learner, is limited and needs to be extended. One of the ways this extending can be encouraged is to enable the participants in education to share their experiences.

One of the most dramatic consequences of this development has been the rehabilitation of the Bible as a fundamental tool in adult religious education, to provoke questions rather than provide superficial and perhaps dangerously inappropriate answers. The remarkable increase of interest in new approaches to adult Bible study and the popularity of Ignatian methods encouraging the employment of imagination and working through to decision making and change in attitude or behaviour are but two obvious results of this realisation.

These are but some of the developments that have enabled adult religious education to break free from an over-concentration on the passive reception of 'input' and become a more dynamic process in which teacher and learner are "bonded and knit together" in a collaborative relationship ("each part working properly"), growing in this relationship together, and building one another up in love. But, this collaborative model has had further implications in that there is a new and increasing focus on the church as an environment for learning and the recognition that the activities associated with adult religious education must involve the whole Church community – the parish and beyond.[15]

IV Implications for the parish – and beyond

FOR THE LOCAL PARISH community the possibilities and opportunities for being more a creative agent in the proclaiming and the bringing in of the Kingdom of God are considerable but have resulted in the emergence of certain points of tension. The broader view of the content and context of Christian education raises questions such as who decides and controls the increasingly complex agenda, challenging the traditional position of the theologian and the theologically trained minister at the helm.[16] Christian lay people with experience and insights from other fields see a place for their expertise in the overall process of Christian development. As Anton Baumohl observes: "At the heart of this is the growing recognition that a theology that helps adults make sense of society, and their own lives within it, involves developing a dialogue between everyday experience and long held Christian truths and doctrines."[17] This focusing on the 'Monday to Friday' experience of lay people as a legitimate locus of Christian discipleship 'in dispersion' highlighted in the report *Called to be Adult Disciples*[18] is but the acknowledgement of the truly sacramental nature of faith, in that it gathers from and permeates all areas of life so that all activities of our lives can become for us means of grace and nurture.

One of the most obvious areas of parish life which focuses this sacramental nature of faith is the celebration of the liturgy when the scattered community of believers gathers to do together those very actions which are the distinctive marks of Christian eucharist: taking, blessing, breaking and distributing. But these actions are the actions not just of the priest at the altar, performing them simply as ritual. They belong to the whole people as marks of the dynamic of their lives, and should therefore be incorporated more dramatically in the liturgy and made more of in reflection on what the liturgy itself is all about. Thus the worship of the parish community becomes a therapeutic encounter with the living God, not only at the moment of communion, but as the recognition and celebration of the presence of the Lord among his people. We have surely only begun to explore the opportunities of making parish worship truly liturgical – the 'work of the people' – rather than a performance put on for the people to observe from a distance.

The greatest of educational treasures the Church has at its disposal is the one most taken for granted and so grossly misused – the Bible. Very little imagination goes in to the actual presentation of scripture in public worship, and the reading of it rarely strikes one as the communication of the words of eternal life. Reading is not the only way in which the message of biblical passages can be communicated, and if we are thinking in terms of effective teaching/learning, surely we should be considering the use of visual elements in the form of drawings, mime, drama, or dance to accompany if not replace reading on occasions. If scripture is meant to inspire, then surely we can attempt to enable people to engage with it in a way that elicits their attention!

Likewise with the exposition of scripture. Here more than anywhere else we have the opportunity to relate the church's story and vision to the stories and vision of God's people, but again we find ourselves locked into patterns which are so counter-productive and inimical to effective learning. Of course there is a place for a good sermon that enables the hearers to engage with the speaker, but what about other ways of getting the message across?

Those parish communities in which the sacramental dimension of life is highlighted and celebrated are at a considerable advantage in an age which puts so much stress on the visual and tangible as vehicles of communication. But here again we can sadly become victims of our past. Signs and symbols can be powerful and evocative but how often do we check to ensure that our ways of using sacramental elements in worship are still conveying the messages we think they are conveying? The most powerful signs communicate directly with no need of lengthy and complex explanations. If we find our signs and symbols cannot be appreciated or recognized for what they are (or for what we think they are!) dare we consider replacing them with others which will communicate more effectively?

One aspect of local parish life which has developed in recent years to great effect is the small group in which participants can build up trust and mutual support. Such groups meeting for Bible study, discussion or other forms of learning can help to overcome many of the negative and inhibiting experiences that people have experienced at earlier stages in life, particularly in school years. Here considerable skill is required to make the most effective use of this more intimate context. The pitfalls, risks and opportunities of these groups are not always obvious and such a context which invites full participation from everyone makes many Church leaders ill-at-ease. Training and preparation for the facilitating (rather than leading!) of such groups is essential and it is at this point that we may well find ourselves having to move beyond the confines of the local parish.

We considered earlier the sometimes daunting demands which are made on local parish personnel, and none is more urgent or insistent than requests for training to acquire expertise. Here, it is more than likely that the local parish leadership will have to look beyond its own community for assistance or advice. Most dioceses or Church headquarters have trained staff whose responsibility it is to advise or offer specific training in most areas of lay ministry and leadership. No longer is it realistic or reasonable to expect people with no experience or training in small group methods to be able to function comfortably and effectively as facilitators or convenors in small group contexts. As more and more lay people experience new learning methods and models in other areas of life so their expectations are raised and they are less inclined to tolerate outmoded or insensitive methods of teaching and learning in the Church.

For those who are looking for something more specialised or beyond the scope of the local parish programme there is a growing number of continuing Christian education networks and centres for adults to which local people can be referred. The advantage of such centres is that they are able to provide, at central locations, learning resources for a viable number of people from a wider area, and enlist the services of specialists who would not be available within the local parish. Another advantage of such centres is of course the opportunity they provide to meet and engage with a wider variety of people, and so benefit from engagement with a greater cross-section of fellow learners. Retreats are another form of Christian nurture beyond the parish and the same advantages pertain.

In recent years, while the revolution in methods of teaching and learning has been going on, many within the church have been oblivious or resistant to its impact. The desire being expressed more insistently by more and more lay people for renewal in the church and particulary in its methods of education is leading "to an increased awareness of those features of its life and structures which are obstacles to learning".[19] Much has been and is being achieved but much still remains to be done to overcome the resistance and reluctance that abound in many local Churches. Professional educators both within and outside the Churches look with considerable misgivings if not dismay on the magnitude of the task to be tackled. There are, however, sufficient signs of hope now that the religious dimension has been re-discovered and reclaimed for adult Christian education programmes and the curriculum tools are avaialable to handle it. The task may be great but the resources are equal to it for those resources are the gifts already given us by the Lord of the Church that "some should be apostles, some prophets, some evangelists, some pastors and teachers, for the equipment of the saints, for the work of ministry for building up the body of Christ."[20]

John Cullen is director of the Institute of Christian Studies, a centre for continuing Christian education for adults, in central London.

The mass media

Peter Verity

ALTHOUGH Christian people in parishes up and down the country are enthused by the *idea* of evangelisation, the actual practice is often somewhat lacking. This has certainly been my experience. I used to travel around the country from parish to parish as part of the Catholic Missionary Society and often asked people to become involved in mission. Invariably the answer came back: "Yes we want to evangelise, but we must get our own house in order first." On returning to the same parish five years later, the answer would still be the same and the mission of the Church would have come no nearer.

Of course, there is some truth in the fact that we need to get our own house in order but there should come a time when we accept our limitations as they are and step out into the big wide world with some Good News. The reticence is understandable, coming, I'm sure, from a natural desire to stay with what is familiar and safe. The step towards mission is the harder option although I firmly believe it is essential for the fullness of Christian life.

The starting point for this article is that we accept that the Church should be engaged in mission. By that I mean that the article is not an attempt to argue the case for Christian involvement in the wider world. That is for another article in another place. This article will explore one of the means of this Christian involvement namely, the media, the content of the message we are trying to proclaim, and the ways in which this is already happening.

The media

IN 1971, a document was published by the Vatican's Pontifical Commission for the Means of Social Communication. It is entitled 'Pastoral Instruction for the application of the decree of the Second Vatican Ecumenical Council on the means of social communication'. While it received little attention outside the circles of the Roman Catholic communicators, for them it has been a text book which is still referred to today. Indeed, it was a document which had such depth that even with all the developments in the world of communications since 1971, the relevance of most of the teaching contained in it is as valid now as it was then. The chapter on the use of the media for giving the Good News (Nos 126–134) seems particularly appropriate for the theme of this article. Number 126 puts it with disarming simplicity:

> Christ commanded the apostles and their successors to 'teach all nations', to be 'the light of the world' and to announce the Good News in all places at all times. During his life on earth, Christ showed himself to be the perfect communicator, while the apostles used what means of social communication were available in their time. It is now necessary that the same message be carried by the means of social communication that are available today.

That is as clear and unequivocal a statement as could be made and a forceful call for Christians to use the mass media. But, the document does not stop there. It goes on to say that using the media is not simply an option, albeit an important one, it is a necessary part of being a Christian. It says:

> Indeed it would be difficult to suggest that Christ's command was being obeyed unless all the opportunities offered by the modern media to extend to vast numbers of people the announcement of his Good News were being used.

Further authority for this comes clearly in Pope Paul VI's encyclical letter *Evangelii Nuntiandi* (Number 45). Writing about the means of evangelisation, Pope Paul says of the mass media;

> When they are put at the service of the gospel, they are capable of

increasing almost indefinitely the area in which the Word of God is heard, they enable the Good News to reach millions of people. The Church would feel guilty before the Lord if she did not utilise these powerful means that human skill is daily rendering more perfect. It is through them that she proclaims 'from the housetops' the message of which she is the depository. In them she finds a modern and effective version of the pulpit. Thanks to them she succeeds in speaking to the multitudes.

The message

HAVING ESTABLISHED that the use of the mass media is essential for Christians, various other questions present themselves. In particular, there will always be discussion as to what exactly the message should be. It is all very well saying it should be the Good News of Jesus Christ, but in a post-Christian society what does this mean?

There are many examples of misunderstanding in this regard. We have only to look at some of the more extreme examples of American tele-evangelism to see how wrong certain interpretations can be. But, it is not simply the extremes that cause problems; among most Christian communicators there is a certain ambivalence. What exactly is it we are trying to give people when we use the mass media to communicate the Good News? Are we trying to tell them the story of Jesus, with no gloss or interpretation? If we are commenting on the gospel story, what criteria do we use to say that our interpretation is the true one? There will always be people who disagree with our interpretation so what authority do we have for our version?

Or perhaps it is really Christian teaching and doctrine that we want to give? But here again, there are differences of opinion on many points not only between denominations but within each denomination as well. Who is going to give the authentic teaching, Hans Kung or Marcel Lefebvre; David Jenkins or Graham Leonard? If it is simply teaching Christian doctrine through the media, we are in a minefield.

There will be some people who believe that the media should be used principally for promoting a particular denomination. As we shall see later, this can be healthy if it simply means giving correct, factual information in response to requests from the media, but at its extreme it can become close to proselytism because it will be promoting a particular Christian tradition in opposition to others.

In *Evangelii Nuntiandi* Pope Paul devotes a whole section to the content of evangelisation (Nos 25–39). It is outside the scope of this article to even begin to summarise this, but one quotation from another part of the document (Number 18) has helped me over the years to understand what I am trying to do when I evangelise and in particular what I am doing in my contact with the media. Pope Paul says:

> For the Church, evangelising means bringing the Good News into all the strata of humanity, and through its influence transforming humanity from within and making it new: "Now I am making the whole of creation new."

Since I encountered that phrase 10 years ago it has shone like the light of a star to guide me to what is true evangelisation.

The means

FACED with all these dilemmas as to the content of the message, it is hardly surprising that many Christians are not able to accept the challenge of using the media for evangelisation. And it is true that until we know what it is we want to say, there's not much point in using valuable time and resources in trying to say it.

But, in spite of that, there are many Christians who are trying to "bring the Good News into all the strata of humanity" through the mass media. I don't want to dwell here on the more extreme examples but to explore some of the practical ways in which the Christian Churches are developing.

At national level, the major denominations have their press or media offices and their own training facilities. The press offices are run professionally and operate in a similar way to the press office of any large organisation. The press offices of the major denominations collaborate well in those matters which need to be dealt with ecumenically. There is an annual residential meeting for all the Churches' national press officers and frequent contact by phone. The task of these offices is twofold. In the first place the task is to respond to calls from the media by giving accurate and concise information about the Church. In practice this means talking to journalists on the phone and explaining the background to stories they are doing. It also involves putting journalists in touch with experts in particular fields and finding suitable people for television and radio interviews.

The other task of the Churches' press offices is to actively promote the values of the gospel and of the Church's teaching. This is the pro-active side of the work and it is evangelisation in the sense of "bringing the Good News into all the strata of humanity". This involves putting out press releases about activities in the Church and planting ideas in the minds of producers and features editors. It is difficult to quantify the success or failure of this task. The only appropriate analogy seems to be the sowing of seeds in a field with very little indication of which seeds have grown.

The work of the national offices can also bear fruit more locally. In the Catholic Media Office we recently held a meeting for all the diocesan information officers of England and Wales. More than 70 per cent of the Catholic dioceses were represented and future meetings are being planned. The day was encouraging to all the participants because they were able to share their difficulties – lack of time, other commitments, lack of expertise – and also to listen to some examples of good practice from the more active dioceses. Among the good ideas which emerged were the publication of press releases to announce the bishop's pastoral letters, a meal with the bishop 'off the record' for the editors of local newspapers, a wine and cheese party for local journalists with key people in the diocese, and a 'media week' in all the schools of the diocese to heighten the awareness of the Christian apostolate in the media. From the national perspective, developing good media officers at diocesan level is a priority because that in turn will lead to further development at parish level.

There is one other aspect of the work of the national media offices which is important to mention. Our task is not just to service the media with information about the Church but also to serve the Church with information gleaned from the media. In technical terms we would say that this is helping the members of the Church to "read the signs of the times". Listening to the world, discerning the movement of the Spirit, and interpreting the signs found in the media are all important parts of the work of Christian communicators. If evangelisation necessarily involves dialogue, and dialogue involves listening, then the Churches must listen to the voices of contemporary society. In practice, this means pointing out certain trends which emerge in the media and being able to influence and modify Church statements so that they will be listened to and understood by the public. The Pastoral Instruction on Social Communications (Number 175) puts it like this:

> It is not enough to have a public spokesman. There must be a continual two-way flow of news and information. On the one hand, this aims to present a true image of the Church in a way that makes it visible to all. On the other, this exchange reveals to the ecclesiastical authorities the surges, currents and ideas that stir the world. Clearly this calls for the cultivation of friendly relations based on mutual respect between the Church, people and groups. In this way continual exchanges can be fostered, with each side both giving and receiving.

A question

THERE IS ONE final question which still needs to be decided within the Churches. One side of the argument thinks that the Churches should be developing their own media in order to teach the nations. The other side thinks that closer involvement in the existing media is more effective as a method of teaching. The Pastoral Instruction does not come down on one side or the other. In Number 132 it says:

> The Church can use means of communication that are not under her control but which, under agreed conditions, are offered for her use. Where it is necessary, she may also herself own and administer means of communication. No hard and fast rules can here be laid down; the situation varies from place to place. Religious authorities will advise those who are involved in this apostolate what to do within the differing conditions of different countries.

In some countries there exist radio and television stations owned by one denomination, and there are daily newspapers which are owned by the Church. This is not true in Britain even in the case of religious press, since these are meant to be for a readership within the Church and do not compete with the national secular news-papers. The main argument in favour of owning these stations or newspapers is that it would give total editorial control so that a true version of the Good News would be presented and they would become real instruments for teaching. The argument against them is that only those committed to the Christian faith would be as ineffec-tive for reaching the vast majority of the population as the Sunday homily.

My own view is that it is more appropriate for Christians to use the existing media and to be there 'in the market place' influencing the mass media. Theologically, I do not believe that we should set up a Christian enclave which is simply for the benefit of adherents. If the definition of Pope Paul is true, we must be bringing the Good News into all the strata of humanity, including all the strata represented in the media. It is not always an easy task to do this and it can lead to misrepresentation and misunderstanding. But, I'm sure that in Britain at least, this is the most effective way forward.

Resources

WHATEVER WAY we choose to be involved in the media for Christian education, resources of money and personnel must be put in. It is not necessarily the cheap option to say we will not set up our own television or radio station or put up our own satellite, expensive as these things may be. If the same sort of resources were to be put into trying to influence the existing media from within, we would be making true progress. These resources need to be used to train people to be effective communicators and to develop a sensitivity to the media among Church members.

At the end of the Pastoral Instruction there is a rather quaint paragraph which helps to illustrate how quickly the world of mass communications is developing:

What is certain is that soon, due to the latest technical developments – especially those that concern communications satellites – sounds, images and the messages they bear will soon be reaching people, simultaneously, all over the world. It will be possible to record these and play them back at will – either for entertainment or for instruction.

As you watch your Sky television or turn on your video recorder, remember that this was only written in 1971. What a long way the technical developments have come in those 18 years!

On a more sober note, can we say that the use of the media by the Christian Churches has developed as quickly? Or are we still where we were in 1971? Having outlined prophetically the technical developments of the future, the Pastoral Instruction gives its prophecy of the possible Christian response:

> So it will be possible for all people to learn more of each other as a result of this real dialogue. They can then work together for the unity of mankind and the establishment of peace. Suddenly, and in proportion with these changes, the responsibilities of the People of God will enormously increase. Never before will they have been offered such opportunities. It will be possible to ensure that the media promote the advancement of the whole human race and the development of those countries in what is called the Third World. It will be possible to strengthen the brotherhood of man. And then the Good News can be given everywhere, bearing witness to Christ, the Saviour.

Let us hope that the Churches will fulfil that prophecy as effectively as the technicians have fulfilled theirs.

Peter Verity is a Roman Catholic priest and director and press officer of the CMO, the Catholic Media Office.

The Church in Education

Peter Pilkington

THE MORAL EDUCATION of most early peoples was customary in character. From the *Iliad* and the *Odyssey* the Greeks drew lessons in such virtues as piety, hospitality, courage, temperance and self-control. Formal and informal educational agencies, the school and public opinion – all united to inculcate and enforce these moral virtues. Religion, too, added its sanctions to ensure that the youth would grow up in virtuous habits. The style of this teaching was authoritarian. Yet, the Greeks were the first to break from this rigidity of religious and moral education in the Sophists who tried to teach morality through a critical analysis of custom and conventions. Aristotle criticised this rational and critical approach. To possess knowledge about morals, Aristotle claimed, was not enough; one must practise morals as well. One must form moral habits. With the help of a teacher a child tries to realise his potentialities for good.

The early Christian Church shared Aristotle's views. Like Aristotle St Paul was sceptical of the Sophist view of education, particularly the view that to know right was to do it for, as he pointed out, although we know the better we often do the worse. The Christian Church had a pessimistic view of human nature and one of the main objects of education was the restoration of man in the image of God. Hence the Church took a decisive role in education and throughout the Middle Ages education kept its eye steadily on eternity and super-mundane affairs. Yet, the work of St Thomas Aquinas (1225–74) in his *Summa Theologica* shows that this approach did not prohibit creative thinking, in that the *Summa* represents an imaginative attempt at a synthesis of the revived classical and Aristotelian philosophy and Christian revelation.

In the fifteenth and sixteenth centuries interest in mundane affairs paralleled interest in the other worldly. This humanism defined itself by the study of the classics but the Church was still a powerful force in education. The fourteenth and fifteenth centuries had seen a growth of the lay spirit but it was still felt that education had an important part to play in the development of a Christian personality. Few schoolmasters of the sixteenth and seventeenth centuries doubted their role as teachers of Christian virtue. When Dean Colet founded St Paul's School, in 1509, the High Master was to be learned in Latin and Greek literature but also to "be to them a master not only of grammar but virtue". The motto of his new school was *Fide et literis*. Thus, godliness and good learning were seen as essential parts of the educational process and David Newsome begins his book *Godliness and Good Learning* with the following dialogue.

'What is a college without a chapel?" Bishop Christopher Wordsworth once asked a friend who was a canon of Winchester Cathedral. 'An Angel without wings,' was the prompt reply.[1]

The union of education and religion was still strong in the nineteenth century and only a few questioned the ideal that training in moral and Christian virtue was an integral part of the educational process.

Yet, even while Arnold was saying that "instruction as applied to the young goes under the name of education; as far as it regards persons of all ages it generally takes the form of religion", society was being transformed by the forces of secularism. The roots of the secularism which came to dominate society remain the subject of dispute. The enlightenment of the eighteenth century with its optimistic view of human nature, combined with David Hume's attack on objective moral principles as embodied in an idea of natural law, laid the roots of the idea that man is complete in himself and patterns of morality and education must be formed within this philosophy. The sheer success of the industrial revolution in a material sense, together with the lessening of social bonds as a result of urbanisation, all strengthened this feeling. The discoveries of Darwin, showing a nature "red in tooth and claw", further weakened faith in an orderly, moral universe and a personal God. In 1902–03 R. Mudie-Smith did a survey for the *Daily News* to show the number of people in the

LCC who went to Sunday worship and found only 832,051 out of a population of 4,470,304 attended a service (i.e. about two out of eleven).

The 1870 Act established a state educational system though the denominational schools (mainly Anglican) were left untouched in those areas where they were working well. In these new state schools religious instruction should "exclude any catechism or religious formulary distinctive of any particular denomination". The English state schools, unlike those of France and the USA, still allowed religious instruction though of a non-confessional style.

The Church in the nineteenth century had largely opposed state involvement in education. In the 1850s Archdeacon Denison had said: "So long as the civil power would help the spiritual power to do God's work in the world on those terms of which alone the spiritual power could be the fitting judge . . . . it ought to be thankfully received . . . . The school of the English parish is the nursery of Catholic truth and apostolic discipline." And the Revd W. Sewell said simply and directly: "The state shall not without a creed without a sacrament, and without any ministerial authority from God, undertake to educate the people of this country." Non-denominational teaching in terms of the 1870 Act was anathema to most Anglicans. The ideal pattern for Anglo-Catholic parishes of the late nineteenth century was a school closely associated with the Church, and sometimes staffed by nuns. The ideology of many in the Church with regard to education was still based on the feeling that education must be guided by the principles and morals revealed in scripture as interpreted by God's Church. Even in the nineteenth century many liberal clergy opposed this view and for several years the annual meetings of the National Society were the scene of pitched battles between liberals and high churchmen. Liberals accused the high churchmen of preferring to keep children in ignorance rather than let them receive light not tinted by themselves. The practice of the Church from 1870 to the start of the Second World War was to fight hard for the continuance of their denominational schools and there were often bitter battles between non-conformists and Anglicans, particularly around 1914 when Welsh disestablishment aroused sectarian passion.

Yet, up to 1939, although many deplored these denominational battles, the idea of schools tied to the Church was still attractive to many Anglicans. Church training colleges felt they existed to send committed Anglicans into Church schools, and almost all colleges expected their students to be regular communicants and Chapel was often compulsory.

The 1944 Act ushered in the era of voluntary aided schools and agreed syllabuses. In aided schools the Church provides 15% of the cost of new buildings and foundation (Church appointed) governors control the governing body. The teachers are paid by the local authority which also provides equipment and maintenance. The governors of such a school would have the right to appoint staff, control the use of the building for non–school purposes, decide the pattern of religious instruction, and subject to national educational policy organise the curriculum and determine admissions policy. Thus an aided school is in effect controlled by the Church and could see its role as designing a pattern of education within the framework of Church teaching. The voluntary controlled school (created by the 1944 Act) would be maintained wholly by the local authority and the Church would have no responsibility for buildings though they would remain the property of the providing body. Only one third of the governing body would be appointed by the Church and religious instruction would be according to the agreed syllabus.

All Roman Catholic schools are aided, but the majority of Anglican schools are voluntary controlled. In 1981 there were 7,935,697 children in maintained schools. There were 863,279 children in Church of England schools (10.9% of the total) and of these 467,813 (5.9%) were in controlled schools and 395,466 (5.0%) in aided. However, only 154,349 were in C of E secondary schools and of these only 89,891 were in aided schools. The Roman Catholic Church had 727,176 pupils in its schools (all aided) and of these 346,406 were in secondary schools.

It can be seen from these figures that the Anglican and Roman Catholic Churches have, since 1944, followed different policies with regard to education. The Church of England has not felt that denominational education should be maintained at all costs and her aided schools form only 7.5% of the primary sector and 2.3% of the secondary. In contrast the Roman Catholic Church has vigorously supported its denominational aided schools which form 9.3% of the primary sector and 9.0% of the secondary. A majority of the children of practising Roman Catholics are educated in schools controlled by the Church. Further, the Roman Catholic Church has made every effort to see that its schools are available in most areas of the country where there are substantial Catholic populations. This is not the case with Anglican aided schools, and over large areas of the country the children of practising Anglicans are educated either in maintained or voluntary controlled schools.

The Anglican view seems to argue that the best way for Christians to temper the forces of secularism and materialism in society is for a partnership between the State and the established Church, in which the Church influences the State educational system by participation rather than control of its own schools. In many ways this reflects the ethos of an establishment in creating a Christian Commonwealth though many might say we are neither Christian nor Commonwealth.

In a Green Paper published in 1984 the National Society set out the ideals of a Church school either aided or voluntary controlled and these show clearly how they see the Churches' role as the leaven in the lump of a largely secular society. They talk of the school being a safe place where there is no ideological pressure, an ecumenical nursery creating a sensitivity to other faiths, a place of distinctive excellence extending further than the narrowly academic. They also stress membership of the community, Christian relationships and the encouragement of creativity. They feel no guilt at this sharing of common ground with secular humanism or that it might not represent the ideals of Christians working in state schools and they write "if . . . . practice corresponds closely to the practices of secular colleagues, the Christian teacher must be profoundly grateful that he is able to share common ground and he will resist the temptation to claim for his own practice a Christian distinctiveness in which secular colleagues cannot share" and virtue is seen in "schools being cradles of healthy pluralism". This view is optimistic and mirrors some of the rationalism that characterises the thoughts of Socrates and some of his contemporaries. Socrates had claimed that no one would knowingly do what was wrong. To think oneself through to the whole truth about the good one must approach it from many different individual angles. To arrive at the universal, moral education must proceed on the presupposition that the human mind is the channel for universal reason. It's doubtful if the National Society would claim Socrates as a patron but Anglican thinking since 1944 has a hopeful optimism which expresses itself in the idea that service and idealism will draw from society virtues which are inherently Christian and that this may lead to faith. The best is there and only needs drawing out. 'Leaven in the lump', 'suffering servant', 'service' exemplify this thinking in the established Church and its part in the educational process. It certainly would not satisfy Archdeacon Denison. The idea of human nature within this philosophy is far from pessimistic and it reinforces many trends in our society.

The essence of Christianity is that God revealed himself in Jesus, whose presence continues throughout time in the Church and its sacraments. The gospel is making an arrogant claim that truth has been revealed and the task of the Church is to present it to the world. The secularist idea that the world is complete in itself denies any idea of God or of incarnation. Further, there is a strong prejudice in modern thinking against any objective creed. There are no absolute values in morals or belief and all truth is relative and varies in different cultures and eras. Inevitably, education reflects society's ideas and the creeds of our time influence educational ideas. Education has been affected by the ideas of Rousseau: "Give the child the wish and . . . . any method will then be suitable", and "Hold childhood in reverence and do not be in any hurry to judge it for good or ill . . . .Give nature time to work before you take over her business and interfere in her workings." Ideas of relative values, and doubts about structures incline modern educators to mistrust any idea of imposing patterns of belief and morals on the educational process. A dilemma exists for Christians who believe in revealed truth in that some feel that the materialistic and individualistic forces in society are so strong that the Anglican policy of partnership and infiltration only means the abandonment of organising education according to the truths of revelation. Yet, there is still a strong body of opinion that thinks that it is better to have a Christian influence on the whole of education, rather than restrict the Churches' activity to specifically Church schools as is done by the Roman Catholic Church.

These educational difficulties reflect the problems that the Christian Church faces in the late twentieth century. We exist in a pluralist society which instinctively mistrusts any idea of an objective truth. There is also doubt as to the value of imposing authoritarian schemes of belief and morals on individuals. Many argue that each person should discover his own pattern of belief and morals rather than have a system imposed upon them. These arguments affect attitudes to issues like divorce and baptism; and, in essence, concern the manner of the Church's existence and mission in the world. The Church of England established by law has for centuries seen part of its mission as service to the State. This tradition has governed its policy towards education, but the changes in society have made this particular task more difficult. Many Catholic and Evangelical Anglicans feel that faith has been diluted, and religious belief has been sacrificed to humanist values. It may be that building in love requires the Church to consider the policy of the Roman Catholic Church here and in Europe. Whether to be "leaven in the lump" or a "city set on a hill" – these are the great issues for the Church today, and the answers we make will decide the nature of our Church in the next century.

Peter Pilkington is an honorary canon of Canterbury Cathedral and High Master of St Paul's School, Barnes, London.

The importance of religious education in our schools

Kenneth Baker

THE OPENING SECTION of the Education Reform Act says that the school curriculum must promote the spiritual, moral, cultural, mental and physical development of pupils at the school and of society. This represents the foundation of our curricular reforms.

Considerations of values affect every aspect of adult life-citizenship; home life and parenthood; care for those who are weaker than ourselves; enterprise and employment. One of the things that each one of us has to do as we move through life is to develop a sense of values. That has to be set within a clear moral framework which allows children and adults to distinguish between right and wrong. If a society cannot define those boundaries clearly it will not have the clarity of purpose, nor the belief in its own essential soundness, to sustain it amongst the pressures and temptations of the world.

A clear moral framework provides certainty and gives both to the individual, and to the country in which they live, a self-confidence.

It was not surprising therefore that many of the debates on the Education Reform Bill reflected the view that moral values could be imparted in a much better way in our schools. In several of the debates, anxiety was expressed about the fact that in recent years the moral and spiritual dimension of education had been watered down. When I spoke to the General Synod earlier this year I set out eight simple moral values. They are not comprehensive but they seem to me to be essential ingredients for any civilised society to progress in harmony.

Four describe things that are wrong: to lie, to steal, to cheat and to bully. Four describe what is right: to respect your elders, to know that you can't have everything you want instantly, to take personal responsibility for your own actions and, above all, to help those less fortunate, and those weaker than ourselves.

These can be taught or imparted to children in many ways. And, let there be no doubt that, in my view, this has to start in the home. Parents are the first educators of children. They should not shrug off their responsibility and expect teachers to do what they have failed to do. But, teachers and schools have a vital role in partnership with parents.

This is why the Religious Education and collective worship proposals in the Education Reform Act are so important. They restate the provisions of the 1944 Act and build upon them. It represents a historical strengthening of the position of RE and worship in our schools.

It provides new opportunities not only for schools to improve and invigorate their Religious Education and collective worship, but also for the Churches to become more engaged with schools. Take for example the fact that all local authorities are now required, rather than simply empowered, to set up a Standing Advisory Council on RE, SACRE.

The Act also reflects the government's belief that proper regard should be paid to our nation's Christian heritage and traditions, in the content of both the worship and RE in schools. That was certainly the intention behind the 1944 Education Act. However, concern was expressed in the House of Lords during the debate on the Bill that the Christian element in worship and Religious Education had diminished and, in some cases, had virtually disappeared.

The Government recognised this concern in supporting amendments to the Act introduced by the Bishop of London. The amendments were the result of detailed consultations by the Bishop with the Catholic and Methodist Churches, with representatives of other faiths, and with teachers' and parents' organisations.

The ERA describes RE as part of the "basic curriculum" for all pupils. It has to be there. But RE is not part of the National Curriculum and its contents will not be laid down from the centre by the secular bodies which have been set up to determine the details of the other subjects in the National Curriculum.

The ERA says nothing new about RE in aided schools, which will continue to be in accordance with the school's trust deed or the custom of the school. Existing voluntary aided schools will continue with their own particular approach to Religious Education. They still give a much greater emphasis to RE which usually infuses the ethos of the schools and makes them so popular.

As regards RE in county schools, and for many pupils in controlled schools, Parliament has said that new agreed syllabuses must "reflect the fact that the religious traditions in Great Britain are in the main Christian whilst taking account of the teaching and practices of the other principal religions represented in Great Britain."

I think this strikes the right balance. It is difficult to understand our history and to appreciate our society today without recognising the effect that Christianity has had upon us. Indeed many parents who have given up practising as Christians nonetheless feel much happier if their children are brought up in schools where real values are imparted. It is usually quite easy to recognise where those values are reflected in the personal behaviour of the children towards their teachers, parents and the other children in the class.

The 1944 Act also provided that all pupils should take part in a daily act of collective worship, unless they were withdrawn by their parents. This has been re-enacted but with new flexibility in how daily worship is organised.

The content of the collective worship in voluntary schools is not affected by the ERA. It continues to be such as is required by the school's trust deed, or by the custom of the school. For county schools, however, there is a new requirement that worship should be "wholly or mainly of a broadly Christian chara er". This does not mean that all individual acts of worship should be Christian, but most acts in any term must be so.

The Act also acknowledges that, in some county schools, or for some pupils at such a school, Christian worship would not be appropriate. In such circumstances it will be open to the head teacher to apply to the local SACRE to relieve the school as a whole, or in respect of those pupils, from the duty to provide worship which is wholly or mainly Christian. Where this duty is lifted, the school still has a responsibility to provide collective worship for the pupils involved. This may not be distinctive of any particular denomination but may be distinctive of a particular faith.

The government hopes that head teachers will not be hasty in making applications to SACREs. I believe that there is advantage in the whole school worshipping together as a community, if that can be arranged.

RE and collective worship are unique in the school curriculum in that parents are allowed to withdraw their children from them. The right of withdrawal is given because many parents feel strongly about their commitment to their own religion and do not want their children taught about other religions or denominations, or to worship according to the practices of other religions. The right must be respected and schools must be able to comply with it.

The importance of religious education and collective worship for the children of Britain is as great now as it has ever been, and there will be many opportunities to improve and strengthen it over the next few years. The changes in the Act provide great opportunities for the clergy in all the Christian Churches in Britain.

The Government is confident that the ERA offers a framework which will secure the central place of Christianity within Religious Education and collective worship in schools, while taking fully into account the needs and aspirations of the many people who hold different beliefs.

For all children of whatever faith there is a need to establish a clear sense of values which will guide them through their lives. There is also a need to awaken the spiritual dimension that lies within them.

Kenneth Baker is Chancellor of the Duchy of Lancaster and formerly Secretary of State for Education.

Enemies of joy

Martin Dudley

EARLY in the twelfth century Anselm of Canterbury corresponded with Walram, Bishop of Naumburg. The letters were concerned with some questions of sacramental theology, but they were set into the historical context of the Investiture Controversy and the Gregorian Reform. Walram had been an early supporter of the Emperor in the Controversy and at first Anselm hesitates to address him as "most beloved and reverend Bishop". Assured of Walram's loyalty to the ill-fated Pope Paschal II, his second letter, of 1107, is addressed with "greeting, reverence, prayers, and the affection of love". Walram had set out his dilemma. God, he says, is undivided Trinity, and all who are in God are one in him. Diversity in the Church is directly opposed to unity, and that which proceeds against itself by dissension among its parts cannot stand for long. His particular questions concern diversity in the way in which the eucharist is celebrated and he asks how, as the rite of sacrifice was received from the ancient Fathers, novelty could have crept into the house of God. He dissents from Christ who tends towards diversity, writes Walram. Christ is the way on which we should walk, he whom we should imitate. He who wanders away from Christ walks in peril. And again, it is greatly harmful to the unity of the Church to differ in the matter of the sacraments, and to allow whatever one pleases.

Anselm had occupied the chair of St Augustine since 1093. He was well acquainted with controversy and his disputes with King William Rufus had frequently been violent. It must be reasonable to assume that he was acquainted with Bede's *Ecclesiastical History* and, in particular, with the reply given by Gregory the Great to Augustine's question concerning the variation in the customs of the Churches. Gregory had recalled that Augustine was familiar with the usage of the Roman Church, in which he had been brought up. But, if you have found customs, wrote the Pope, whether in the Church of Rome or of Gaul, or any other that may be more acceptable to God, I wish you to make a careful selection of them, and teach the Church of the English, which is still young in the Faith, whatever you have been able to learn with profit from various Churches. Things should not be loved, he said, for the sake of places, but places for the sake of good things and he called on Augustine to select from each of the Churches whatever things he found to be devout, religious, and right and to bind them together into a sheaf.

Perhaps it is with this in mind that Anselm tells Walram that it would indeed be good and praiseworthy if the sacraments were celebrated in one way and with one mind in the whole Church. Many of the diversities do not conflict with the substance of the sacrament nor with its efficacy nor with faith in it. These, he thinks, should rather: "be peacefully tolerated in union of hearts than be scandalously condemned with discord. For we have it from the holy Fathers that, provided the unity of charity in the Catholic faith is preserved, a different practice does not harm." And from where does diversity come? From the diversity of human dispositions, answers Anselm, able to think of no other place.

These difficulties have a familiar feel as we consider our own position in the Church today. They reinforce the simple and incontestable historical fact that medieval Christendom was not monolithic and they remind us that there never was a golden age that lacked only the questions, controversies and fierce disputes that can be so easily perceived as enemies of our Christian joy. Anselm was deeply involved, we might almost say embroiled, in dispute after dispute, and yet he produced theological and spiritual writings of lasting importance. The controversies took their toll in terms of energy. There was often risk of physical injury, as Anselm's great and martyred successor was to learn. There was also an intensity about living the Christian life that was a stimulus to great works.

We may not feel that the controversies of the second half of the twentieth century have generated the same sort of great works. Of course, we are not the people to judge that; yet I cannot help thinking that our wrestling with so many of the pressing issues of the day is generating not only countless ephemeral reports of merely passing value but also some more solid thinking. I shall try in a moment to substantiate that view, but I want to begin biographically. I don't do this because I think my life and experience is particularly unusual or fascinating, but because I am persuaded that too much theology involves a division between the doctrinal system and religious experience. That division can split my praise and praying, my experience of sin, grace and forgiveness, my spirituality from my thinking, my systematic reflection upon God's revelation and the Christian tradition and from my writing. That split is obvious in many of the polarised debates that characterise the current life of the Church. We hear supposedly objective theological speeches that are marked by undisclosed and perhaps unrecognised subjective judgements and prejudices and they are countered by impassioned pleas that are so divorced from objective reflection that we risk making decisions on the basis of feeling and intuition alone. We should not be subjected to this either/or approach, not least because it denies the unitary nature of our human existence. What we need is a reintegration of our fully-human experience, whether explicitly religious or not, and our reflective articulation of it. We must surrender neither to pure subjectivity nor to the false objectivity which deprives doctrine of its basis in history and which can be, and often is, an escape from the world we do not understand into the realm of eternal truths.

Who I am in the fullness of my humanity, how I came to be what I am, and how I reason theologically cannot be separated. Theology, as Gregory showed in his letter to Augustine, need not lack rigour and insight merely because it is also, or primarily, personal and pastoral. When I say that I shall be autobiographical, I do not mean to burden you with the details of childhood and youth, a Baptist childhood, a youth that followed the expected conversion at a Billy Graham rally, the unexpected movement towards catholicism symbolised by a gold-edged black-leather edition of à Kempis, the discovery of Leeming's *Principles of Sacramental Theology* as a precocious teenager, and my ultimate conversion, after a flirtation with Newman's Oratory, to an Anglo-Catholicism already in turmoil. A list of dates and events will only hint at why Karl Rahner, after Tillich, was the formative influence on my theology and Sydney Evans on my spirituality, why I habitually turn to Aquinas for answers and why I think I shall never join the Roman Church whose theology delights me, and say nothing of the word of grace addressed to me that brought me first to faith and brought me back again when my denial of the divine order had come perilously close to being my "no" to God. A fuller biography would give a clearer idea of why certain questions have attracted my attention, particularly those in the area of sacramental theology. They have been imposed. They have sprung from my experience, from my searching, from my affirming *this* and denying *that*. I hope as well, as Metz says of Rahner, that I have also been open to the needs and questions of others. My questions or their questions, they come together into what Tillich calls the method of correlation, that is, the correlation between existential questions and theological answers.

The enemies of joy, the controversies that disturb the tranquillity of our lives, are precisely these existential questions and their theological answers. A woman asks what ministry God calls her towards. Her answer is uncomfortable, first for her and then for the Church. She has not asked the question idly, and a stock answer will no longer do. A homosexual ponders the sinfulness of a relationship given full genital expression and asks how it can be wrong when all that is good in him is bound up in it. A couple approach the parish priest who has baptised their children, frankly admit that they are not married but both recently divorced, and ask if he will marry them. To reply that the Church will not allow it but that he will cheerfully bless their union is not in fact to face the existential question of the true and Christian or false and adulterous nature of their marriage. I hope that it is not a truism to say that life imposes the theological agenda and that life is frequently uncomfortable.

I should mention another form of controversy, the enemy of joy in many a parish. My successor in my late parish found, as I had also done, that some people no longer came to the worship of the Church because they had fallen out with me or my predecessor. There are always many reasons for that falling out. The new vicar may be too forceful in expressing the teaching of Christ, providing answers to people who have not yet asked the questions and, because they are pressed, never will. Change, liturgical, theological, spiritual and social, may be badly managed. One lady complained to the bishop because I had taught at her child's baptism that spiritual wealth was more important than material wealth and she thought I was getting at her, and perhaps I was. In the parishes we face existential questions because clergy and parishioners are human beings called to live the Christian life. There will be differences because of that diversity of human dispositions affirmed by Anselm. There will be anger, misunderstanding, temptations and opportunities for complaint, though we know how good and lovely a thing it is when brothers, and sisters, dwell together in unity. To maintain that unity we need to think more carefully about criticism and community and to recognise that a seemingly minor issue may camouflage a major question about our humanity. I think, for example, of the storm that raged over artificial flowers in the churchyard and marble gravestones and what was really being said about life and death and the role of the Church on the boundary between them.

Why do we see so many of these questions and answers as enemies of joy? Why do we not embrace them as signs of a healthy diversity in the life of the already diverse (and fragmented) Church? Why are we not content to live, as David Jenkins would have us live, with questions? I have tried living with questions. It is terribly uncomfortable. Questions require answers. They cry out for them. Aristotle's first principle expressed in the *Metaphysics* is that all men, all human beings, by nature, desire to know. And, our answers, if they are to make sense to us, have to be ordered, structured, coherent. We look for consistency and we do not expect mutually contradictory positions to be held at the same time. The positions we have already taken up, explained biographically, are also put into question, and because they are almost certainly part of our self-definition, that putting into question is a painful experience. Not just those who seek change but those who deny it are answering the existential question. The person who denies that a woman can be, now or ever, a priest is answering a question. So are those opposed to any Christian acceptance of homosexual behaviour or marriage after divorce whilst the previous spouse is living. The person who refuses to participate in a modern language service, to share the peace, to receive communion from a woman, or to drink coffee in a church building can presumably justify those actions. The structured order of their knowledge, the coherence of answers to diverse questions, provides this justification. Allow women to be ordained and there is

113

a shift in your doctrine of order or eucharist or God or humanity or all four. To accept homosexuality in any form or remarriage or modern language or a whole variety of other things involves similar more or less radical shifts. It was not by accident that Walram's question began from an affirmation about God.

The questions that disturb, or enrich, the life of the Church are posed by our being human, created, and redeemed, and emerge from our lived experience of the gospel. Although the answer is shaped by that experience, it cannot come from my existential situation alone. I pose the question, but I cannot be the answer. I am also the hearer of the saving word addressed to me by God, the word that comes from outside of me and that is given to me. As the word is independent of me, and yet addressed to me, so the answer has to be both independent of me and related to my question. The task of theology is to bring existential question and theological answer – here I follow Tillich again – within the theological circle. Here the theologian must struggle. Here there is no place for arrogance. There are no glib, easy answers as we correlate the divine revelation and the question posed by the human predicament. The only authentic answer comes from me in the totality of my being, from the questioning of the question in the light of previous decisions which have made me who I am. Although this task may be exhilarating, the response to the existential question must, if it is to be authentic, disturb the peace. It must be an enemy of joy, albeit a welcome enemy.

The unwelcome enemy is the unreflective sub-theology, the amalgam of half-grasped theological religious and anthropological (sociological/psychological) notions underlying much that passes for argument in controversy. The philosopher Stephan Körner has effectively demonstrated how a person's beliefs and practice and pure attitudes are organised. Such organisation leaves room for a great variety of internally consistent, but mutually inconsistent, systems of beliefs and attitudes. The way in which we think about material objects, persons, minds and bodies, social relations, history and science reveals the interrelation of these systems, together with the dominant and subsidiary principles that govern our thinking. The same complexity is to be found with theological thinking, although I hope that there is a greater consistency and coherence of thought among those of us who purport to be theologians. We might well credit this confusion in holding mutually inconsistent beliefs and trying to argue from them to lack of catechesis and a failure in Christian education and formation, but this is the concern of other writers in this volume. The consequence of it, however, is more clear. It is a breeding ground for division, disunity and disregard for Christian charity in dealing with one's opponents. Without exaggeration, we may realistically speak of sin in such a situation. To avoid sin, we must maintain that principle of charity that tolerates diversity and that, even in fierce controversy, accepts the good faith of those with whom we disagree, unless there is clear evidence of malicious intent. And, we shall need a prudent spirit of discernment if we are to know when the disturbance of our joy comes from a "no" to God rather than from a genuine desire to perceive his will and affirm it.

I chose Anselm's correspondence with Walram to begin this essay because it contains many of the ingredients of current controversy. This is yet more obvious when we put it into context. We find Rupert of Deutz, for example, tackling the problems of the Investiture Controversy with theological skill and pragmatic action. His bishop, even though suspected of simony, was still his bishop whose authority he had to accept. But, he was not going to be ordained by him in case the ordinations of simonacs were not valid. He and his fellow monks had either to ask another bishop to minister to them or to wait for better days! Anselm valued unity as much as Walram. Both saw that the unity of the Church was rooted in the unity of God. But, Walram saw only infidelity in diversity, whereas Anselm tolerated it, even if he didn't actually welcome it, as long as the unity of charity in the Catholic faith was preserved. Anselm is flexible to a degree. What he deplores is the discord that lacks charity and is in consequence scandalous. In his answer we surely find a wisdom that comes from experience, a theology authenticated by a holy life, a firmness that is merciful, as befits a bishop. Another Benedictine, Dom David Knowles, wrote somewhere (and I quote it from memory) that the greatest justice is to be found in the deepest sympathy with erring and straying men. Only when we sympathise with those whose disturbing questions we must answer, only when we share fully with them in the human predicament and do not attempt escape into dogmatic truth divorced from Christian living, will the enemies of joy be seen as invitations to a deeper and more authentic life, fully human and fully Christian.

Martin Dudley, Vicar of Owlsmoor in Berkshire, is a theologian, liturgist and writer.

Church government and administration: idol – or tool?

Derek Pattinson

FOR A SIZEABLE number of Church people – including many clergy – it seems that "the times are out of joint". For some there has, in the past 30 years, been too much change; and they fear that there will be more of it, and that it will be even worse. For others the past 20 years in particular have been a period of frustration, of little or no achievement, of marking time and, indeed, of going back after the heady sixties. Each will have his or her own grounds for complaint. On specifics they will often cancel each other out. But, there is a common cause in which many of them come together – condemnation of synodical government, after 20 years of it, and with the attendant bureaucracy and administration. If only, it is said, the General Synod would meet less frequently and would do less, the Church could be free of the burgeoning bureaucracy, and all would be released for the *real* work of the Church.

I have lived too close to the central administration of the Church of England over the past 20 years to be taken in by this convenient, somewhat escapist, myth put about as it periodically is by bishops needing copy for their diocesan leaflets, by crotchety deans and by clergy and laity looking for a whipping boy to beat. Synodical government – the participation of bishops with clergy and laity in the ruling and governing of the Church – is arguably of the *esse* of Anglicanism, even if (as has to be admitted) the Church of England was the last member Church of the Anglican Communion to adopt it. The particular complaints about its English manifestation are not particularly well founded. For example, the General Synod meets on fewer sittings days than did the Convocations and the Church

117

Assembly under the old régime. The central bureaucracy has not grown in numbers since synodical government came in: the General Synod had on its payroll in 1989 fewer people than the Church Assembly had in 1969. The Church Commissioners' staff has fallen back from about 450 to a 1989 figure of under 350. The indications are that the Commissioners' staff numbers will decline further: the trend is towards greater delegation to, and freedom of manoeuvre for, the dioceses. The dioceses have, it is true, acquired more administrative responsibilities such as, for example, the management of glebe. The General Synod took the management of glebe out of the hands of incumbents in the interest of efficient and economical management. There was a great hubbub about the likely cost of administration. But, a handful of dioceses, which ran voluntary schemes ahead of the *Endowments and Glebe Measure*, showed that there need be no great bureaucracy if they took charge. To this day, despite the additional burden laid upon them by the General Synod and by the demands from within the particular diocese, diocesan administrative staffs remain comparatively small – small, certainly, by comparison with local government and even with the private sector professional firms with whom they regularly deal. Perhaps the smack of bureaucracy is felt more heavily simply because mechanisation and computerisation make it easier to ask for, and to analyse, return forms. But, the Central Board of Finance has prided itself in keeping its forms simple – and its statistical staff is smaller today than it was 20 years ago.

If, then, ecclesiastical bureaucracy has *not* burgeoned centrally in the past 20 years, and if increases at diocesan level have been kept to the minimum required for the new – and necessary – tasks which have been assumed, what of the deanery and parish? Deanery synods have no full-time paid staff – only such time as their chairmen and secretaries can spare in the midst of their other duties. There has, on the other hand, been a development of parish staffs. A few city centre parishes, often with civic responsibilities and community work programmes, have long employed a few lay people side by side with the clergy. In other parishes the vicar has had a paid secretary, sometimes full-time but more often part-time. Suddenly, alongside this there have developed a breed of lay, stipendiary, parish administrators. Their task, essentially, is to relieve the clergy of some administrative tasks and to support them and the voluntary lay leadership of the parish in the total ministry. There are some things which often can best be done by a full-time worker. If the clergyman is the only full-timer, such tasks tend to fall to him – and yet, often that is not the best use of his time even if he has the aptitude for them. It may be a by-product of this new lay ministry (for such it is) that parishes find themselves with more paper. At best this is an enrichment: service papers to aid the worship; helpful notices about services, meetings, projects; clear, competently produced agendas and minutes. At worst paper can become a nuisance, a tyrant even.

This leads on to a complaint often made against the General Synod and its agencies – that there is too much paper. There are, it is said, too many reports which no one (or hardly anyone) wants – and that these lead, as the night to day, to the unnecessary but considerable consumption of time in the General Synod and, it may be, in the dioceses and deaneries. This is another area where myths multiply. The truth is that, in general, people see no need for reports on subjects which do not interest them or where they are anxious that there should be no change. A friend spoke to me just as I was sitting down to write this paper. She said that she saw no need at all for *Patterns for Worship*, the latest production of the Synod's Liturgical Commission – responding, as it does, to *Faith in the City* and to an even longer running cry for liturgy expressed (whether in words, or in music, or in action) more simply and directly. My friend has herself no need of such aids to worship. She is highly intelligent and articulate. She likes nothing better than polysyllabic words, which she uses to powerful effect. Moreover, she regards the ASB as an abomination and prefers to stick to 1662 (or, I caddishly suspect, the interim rite). But, in the 1960s and 1970s, the Church of England responded to the liturgical movement which was sweeping through western Christendom; and, who dare say that the compiling of ASB 1980 was other than a response to the Spirit, even if my friend doesn't like any of it and even if I don't necessarily defend every jot and tittle of it?

Again, many Church people, including some Synod members, would have preferred not to be burdened with *Faith in the City* and with the things which have flowed from it. But, the Archbishop of Canterbury commended it and secured for it the support of the

Synod and its Standing Committee, and the result has been *both* the focusing of Church interest and concern in an area of mission where the Church of England's past track record has not been good, and (we can fairly claim) the encouragement of a renewed public (and governmental) interest in inner-city problems. Even more important, in my view, has been the way in which *Faith in the City* has brought the Church of England face to face with the existence, the needs, the contribution and the potential of its black members. In 1990 there is likely to be a report on rural issues – with, I have no doubt, a similarly compelling justification.

Two things need to be kept in mind. First, the range of the reports produced by the General Synod depends upon and reflects the range of its concerns. The Synod is the Church's legislative body; it has powers in relation to liturgy and doctrine; it deals generally with the central business of the Church (those financial and administrative matters which concern the whole Church and not just the dioceses individually); and, it deals with the Church of England's relationships with the Anglican Communion and with other Churches at home and abroad. This work is necessary. Much of it can only proceed properly if it is underpinned by reports and other texts.

But, the General Synod also concerns itself with public issues, in which it addresses itself to government and to the wider community. Some people regret this. They think that the Synod should keep off such issues and, by implication, out of politics. But, some of the issues which the General Synod takes up are issues on which the Christian Church surely ought to – and still, in our society, is expected to – speak out, not only to Church people but also much more widely? Moreover, the Church cannot be limited in the public domain to those issues on which government customarily allows a free vote in Parliament. It follows that, on occasion, it must oppose the government of the day. Ought a Church, with a massive stake in, for example, the educational system, reasonably be expected to be mute during the passage of a controversially innovative Education bill? But, if the General Synod is to concern itself with public issues then it must be adequately briefed. If it is right in principle for the Synod to intervene, it would be irresponsible to do so without an adequate basis of fact and argument. It is right, too, that words should be accompanied by deeds. The Church Urban Fund is one particular working out of *Faith in the City*. But, to give effect to it required a coalition of the central administration, of other skills which the Church did not possess and had to "buy in", and of the abounding energy and enthusiasm of people in the dioceses and parishes.

Reports, then, have to be produced to stimulate thought and trigger action. But, do we have too many of them? My impression is that there are fewer of them than there were, for example, in the 1960s. The General Synod has learnt the hard way and is more chary than it was about commissioning them. It is also more careful than at one time about the business which it refers to the diocesan synods. Some matters must be referred: the legislation about the ordination of women to the priesthood is a prime and topical example of a matter on which the General Synod cannot (by its constitution), and ought not as a matter of principle, pronounce finally without consulting the dioceses. Other sensitive matters need not be referred – subject only to sufficient trust between the different levels.

For some people, however, the legal and administrative incubus is perceived not so much in terms of the General Synod and its deliberations, but in relation to buildings. Do we not have too many churches, halls and vicarages – many of them, to make matters worse, too big or in the wrong place? Have we not saddled ourselves with a legal and institutional framework which battens this burden of buildings upon us? Is not the General Synod, by implementing the proposals in the Bishop of Chichester's report, making it worse? The difficulty here is two-fold. First, in relation to building, no one in this country is free any more "to do what he will with his own". The ordinary man or woman must have planning permission for alterations to their buildings, and may also need listed buildings consent. The Church of England, like the other Churches, has the benefit of the Ecclesiastical Exemption in respect of church buildings in use; and, when churches become redundant, it has (under the Pastoral Measure) a considerable degree of freedom in disposing of them. But, there is a degree of public accountability – accountability to the whole community – from which we cannot escape, and (in my view) from which we ought not to want to escape. It is an account-ability which, not surprisingly, is the more pressing upon us because, for historical and other reasons, the Church of England has in its ownership many of the best medieval buildings which have come down to us, a good deal of the best which come from the sixteenth, seventeenth and eighteenth centuries, and even some of the best work of the nineteenth and twentieth centuries.

Even so, we could still if we wished slim down the number of buildings in use for worship, transferring those not needed for use other than worship but not in conflict with their history and ethos. But, here is the second catch. Our own legislation, which Parliament has approved but which we originated, provides a whole battery of protection for "interested parties". In the end, if we are honest, must we not admit that it is *other people's* buildings, the churches of parishes other than our own, which we would slim down?

Finally, there is the question of resources – human and material. It is to the credit of the Church of England that it is still committed to the proposition that it will provide the means to train and, later, to support the ministry of all who are selected by due process for full-time ministry. The House of Laity of the General Synod, in particular, is committed to this cause. Money has thus far been forthcoming, from endowment income but also in steadily increasing proportion from today's Church people. Fewer people, the statistics show, are providing more money. It is generally reckoned that people will give more readily if they know the use to be made of their gift. People give readily for stipends. Some people say that there is reluctance on the part of parishes to provide money for central, General Synod activities. It is true that dioceses are wary about the General Synod's requests for money. But, in practice, the costs of the General Synod's activities, averaged out at parish level, are comparatively small – and it is the diocese which makes the large claim. Overall, it has to be said that levels of giving in the Church of England are still generally behind those of other Churches in England and of other provinces in the Anglican Communion.

Those who kindly invited me to contribute to this symposium suggested a list of matters to do with the government and administration of the Church where frustration is felt. I have sought in this essay to suggest that, item by item, much of this frustration is misdirected. But, if there is frustration after 20 years of synodical government, and undoubtedly there is, to what does it relate?

To my mind, the answer does not lie so much in the "failure" of synodical government, but rather in its "success". The General Synod, in 20 years, has achieved a great deal which it would be tedious to itemise. But, it did not produce the majorities required to endorse the Anglican/Methodist Scheme and the Covenant. It has not produced majorities to give practical application to its judgement that there are cases where a person marrying after divorce should be able to marry in church. It has agonised, and is still agonising, over the ordination of women to the priesthood. If this is "failure", it is because the Synod, whatever some Parliamentarians may say, is so accurately representative: where the Synod has "failed", it reflects deep division in the Church. Instead, then, of blaming the Synod, people should look to the Church which elects it and which it mirrors. That done, for most bishops, clergy and lay people the next step is to get on with "being the Church" in diocese and parish, a task which continues whatever the particular and the local difficulties. But, from some, more is required. Those whom this does not satisfy should not content themselves with indifference but should get into the business of overcoming the divisions in Church and in Synod. There is a General Synod election this year, 1990. It could be a good time for a fresh start, for a fresh attempt to resolve the frustrations of a divided house.

Derek Pattinson is Secretary General of the General Synod of the Church of England and, over many years, an occasional worshipper at St Mary's, Bourne Street.

Reflections on Synod post-Crockford

George Austin

THE TRAGIC SUICIDE of Canon Gareth Bennett and his consequent exposure as author of the anonymous Preface to the 1987–8 edition of *Crockford's Clerical Directory* was a traumatic experience for the Church of England and not least for its liberal leadership. Such an unnecessary death always spreads guilt, and this was shared not only among those senior figures who had criticised him so bitterly but also among the journalists who had hounded him and as much among his friends who had, because of the anonymity, been unable to help him and may inadvertently have added to his pain and isolation.

Since Crockford there have been a few changes, most noticeably in the pattern of senior appointments. Although I had shared Bennett's view on the scandal of nepotism which guided episcopal appointments, I had by the time of the Preface's publication come to believe, in spite of considerable evidence to the contrary, that ours was too superficial a view and that it was the mistaken belief that Liberals held the "middle ground" of the Church of England which had been the major influence in the development of a liberal élite in the higher offices of the Church. The truth is that, far from being the moderate mean, Liberals have shown themselves to be more extreme, more intolerant and much further from grass-roots opinion and expectations than either Catholics or Evangelicals.

With the appointment of men like Michael Turnbull to Rochester, Alan Chesters to Blackburn, Nöel Jones to Sodor and Man, Pat Harris to Southwell and even of George Carey to Bath and Wells, the bench of bishops has begun to gain a flavour more representative of the Church of England, and the new Dean of St Paul's, Eric

124

Evans, extends that to the rarefied realm of cathedrals. Of course, six swallows do not make a summer and it is too soon to know if a change has really taken place or merely a few crumbs thrown to a weary Church. But there has been an effect on the House of Bishops and therefore on the General Synod itself.

It is not simply that the centre of gravity has shifted in its episcopal membership. The more extreme liberal bishops – such as Rogerson of Bristol, Yates of Gloucester, Booth-Clibborn of Manchester (and Jenkins of Durham, too) – have begun to appear more and more isolated, and can no longer expect the automatic support of the less-committed of their peers. It is now no longer sufficient to present some "new liberal thing" to the Synod (often alas no more than yesterday's discarded answers to tomorrow's unrecognised problems) and to expect the unqualified support of all but a handful of the House of Bishops.

In the past, a combination of hearts-and-flowers pleas about the "hurt" which would be caused if the Open Synod Group Liberals did not get their own way (accompanied by the ecclesiastical equivalent of a spoilt child stamping its feet) was sufficient to sway episcopal votes. The clergy were always too hard-bitten for such a technique, and now it works only with the more sentimental members of the House of Laity.

Bennett described the House of Clergy as "the least persuadable part of the General Synod", one which had "consistently refused its consent to measures which would have changed the character of the Church" and which had "thereby become an object of some irritation to the establishment". This of course is nothing new: the clergy's historic rôle as proctors in Convocation has always been to preserve the Church from the wilder excesses of the Upper House, leading in the past to the suppression of Convocation and in synodical times to pleas from the Open Synod Group to change voting methods or to introduce further "special" categories whose representatives would tend to hold the party line – as with the temporary constituency for women deacons.

Garry Bennett was particularly hard on the House of Laity, describing it as a "a House which is not very impressive.":

It relies heavily on a few excellent speakers and its formidable collection of lay academics. In particular the laity's belief that they can deal with theological matters as competently as the clergy is grievously mistaken and often embarrassing. . . . It is evident that the laity are essentially a reactive body; they respond not so much to argument as to appeals; and they have a disposition to vote for that which is recommended by the leadership of the Church.

Here Bennett was too sweeping, for there are certainly members of the laity who can make theological contributions which easily better those made by more than a few members of the other two houses: Oswald Clarke, Margaret Hewitt, John Gummer, Margaret Laird, Helen King and Frank Williams immediately come to mind. But, the overall judgement remains true, that members of the House of Laity "respond not so much to argument as to appeals". And that is a fundamental problem and weakness of the General Synod which nothing subsequent to the Preface has eased.

The vote, in November 1989, by the General Synod in support of the ordination of women to the priesthood is, without doubt, potentially the most destructive, and it has become so precisely because of the theological weakness of the House of Laity. When, in July 1975, the Synod declared that there were "no fundamental objections to the ordination of women", although it did not limit this to theological objections, it is in fact only the theological objections which are or can be fundamental when such a proposal is before the Church. Yet, by the very nature of the House of Laity, it is the theological issues which will hold least sway, and which in fact have passed almost totally without consideration in the years since 1975. Thus, what little dialogue has taken place has been a dialogue between the deaf, and the hard-line and bitter divisions which now exist owe almost everything to this factor.

Opponents continue to be branded as mysogynists and homosexuals (even though gay clergy tend to see women priests as a human rights issue similar to their own), as against all women's ministry (even though many supported the women deacons proposals), and are ridiculed as people living in the past ("stranded like a dead whale" was a recent description by a leading lay Liberal). Often effectively employed in this as well as in other debates is the gentler English version of the Soviet practice of despatching dissidents to mental institutions. This arises first as a mere hint and then is presented as a pastoral concern for those poor members whose opposition to each new thing is because of their "psychological fears" rather than for any reasoned theological argument. It is a disreputable technique and the pain of being on the receiving end is not eased by the knowledge that it is the last desperate ploy of one whose arguments lack any real substance.

Such techniques ought to have no place in Christian debate and it is to the shame of the General Synod that they have become more common and acceptable, inhibiting though they are to real dialogue. Since they are always irrelevant to whatever matter is in hand, it is hard to understand why such a speaker is not called to order, since the Synod's own standing orders make clear that a chairman should do so for "irrelevance" and "unbecoming language".

It is however not only the content of speeches but also the content of the agenda which colours sessions of the Synod. Garry Bennett was highly critical of the Standing Committee whose members (of whom he was one) reported "their almost complete powerlessness". Eight clergy and eight lay members are elected by their respective houses and the system of STV (single transferable vote) ensures that those elected will reflect the respective strengths of the three Synod "parties" – which themselves are a reflection of the attitude of electors in the dioceses (with one caveat – more of that later).

At the last full election in 1985, the clergy elected four Catholics, three Evangelicals and only one Open Synod Liberal; and the laity two Catholics, four Evangelicals and only two Liberals: a total of six catholics, seven evangelicals and only three liberals. By contrast, the previous standing committee had five Liberals as well as two Evangelicals who would normally support their position. In other words the electorate decided democratically to vote for a change of direction in Synod policy. But, as Bennett pointed out: "over against them is a solid block of ex-officio members" who constitute a "payroll" vote on which the Liberal establishment may always rely for nearly total support.

There was anger in the House of Bishops when the Synod refused to reject, in the discussions on the recent Infrastructure Review, a proposal to remove voting rights from the (normally episcopal) chairman of Synod boards, but hopefully that will help to increase the voice of elected members in the process of decision-making without reducing the contribution which such chairman make to debates in the committee. Nevertheless, more power still needs to be given to the Standing Committee both in forward planning and in deciding which matters should or should not come before the Synod. Activists on the staff of a Board still have too much authority to initiate debates on subjects which Synod has not asked to debate and, if attendance is a criterion, clearly does not wish to debate.

More than anything, the proliferation of pretentious motions (often from the Board for Social Responsibility), simply encourages the Synod to think of itself more highly than it ought to think. Its first task is legislation and it is only in this area that it is and should be analogous to Parliament, since Parliament has granted it authority to be a subordinate legislative body. Moreover, its duty in legislation is to oil the wheels of the Church of England to enable it to be more effective in its mission. In other words, it is the stoker in the engine-room rather than the admiral on the bridge.

Its other – minor – function is to consider and express "opinion on any other matters of religious or public interest". Synod's great illusion is not that it is like Parliament in its legislative function, for it is exactly so and must meet three times a year in order properly to fulfil that function. Its illusion is in imagining that it is like Parliament in its second function of expressing opinion. That illusion has not yet become the delusion of grandeur which made the British Council of Churches such a figure of fun, for Synod does not really believe that government and nation wait with fear and trembling for the results of its deliberations. But it must tread carefully: the General Synod does have a duty as the mouthpiece of informed Christian opinion to comment, favourably or otherwise, on issues of public concern, and if it exercises that duty with responsibility and giving primacy to Christian rather than secular contributions, then it deserves that respect which will have influence as its reward. It will help no-one if it simply dresses the secular in ecclesiastical verbiage, while exhibiting all the predictability of the mindless and militant Left.

Most of all the General Synod must listen more closely to the voice of the man and woman in the pew. Now of course the Synod clergy and laity are grass-roots Church members. It is certainly true that there are Christians at the centre of churchy activity whose lives are one long round of national and sometimes international gatherings where they meet the same committed activists time and again, and live in a world for which they claim to speak but from which they are totally divorced. But, on the whole, Synod members do not live on that remote plane, and spend their lives in the daily round of the world just like anyone else. They know the parishes and the people in them: in fact it is probably true that if one were to call out the name of any of the thousands of parishes in the Church of England, at least one Synod member would know something about that parish, and could probably name more than one worshipper there.

Unfortunately, good though the STV voting system is in fairly representing the three main schools of thought in the Church of England, it is less able to bring into the General Synod structure the ordinary middle-of-the-road Anglican – the person who is not a Catholic or an Evangelical or a Charismatic or a Liberal, but who is just Church of England, and is so, solidly and faithfully, from head to foot and from one year to the next. And those who do slip through the net are often patronised or ignored when they attempt to contribute to debate.

Such people in our parishes, men or women, young or old, will accept change which the General Synod authorises so long as it is not too intrusive into the familiar way of things. They will accept worship from the Alternative Services Book so long as it is recognisably C of E. They will sing new hymns but would revolt if the old favourites were displaced at harvest, Christmas and Easter. They might not mind too much if the vicar or curate were female (although they might like it better if she were priest in the next parish!). But they would be horrified to be faced with the remainder of the liberal package: inclusive language, practising homosexual clergy and gay marriage, Durham theology, the endorsement of secular moral standards in place of biblical, and so on.

If the 1990 General Synod election, fought as it will be on the one issue of women priests, returns a Synod which is predominantly, and therefore by nature intolerantly, liberal then it is conceivable that it will begin a legislative process which will change the character of the Church of England so radically that Catholics and Evangelicals will retreat into their respective ghettos. It is the ordinary middle-of-the-road Christians who will be driven away: and they will never return.

Dom Gregory Dix describes how, before 1549, "the great medieval half-christianised bulk of the population had a tradition of mass-going, and perhaps not much more":

> Yet it did bring them to church, and this offered an unparalleled opportunity for teaching them something more. Instead they were compelled to accept not only a totally different conception of worship, but *two* new rites in rapid succession, followed again by two further revolutions in the next six years, each accompanied by conscientious public murders on a nation-wide scale. Is it any wonder that in the general upheaval, the overthrow of traditional sanctities, the bewildering succession of liturgies, the *habit* of churchgoing broke down? And so the greatest opportunity for the effective evangelisation of England that there ever has been was very largely wasted.[1]

The General Synod in July 1989 welcomed the decade of evangelism. How could it do otherwise for that would have been like voting in favour of sin? But it enters that decade unsure of its gospel. Is it the Good News of the Faith once delivered to the saints which Catholics and Evangelicals endorse; or, is it a faith for modern man with the historicity of the New Testament ridiculed or even excised? Does it speak of a God who washes away *my* sin, for which *I* am responsible; or does it reject that individual responsibility and speak only of a world or a creation redeemed? Does it present a Church whose agenda God alone writes; or is the agenda imposed on God by the secular demands of a world which has rejected the sacred?

The Church of England of the 1990s will be faced with more than a bewildering succession of liturgies. If the new revolutionaries have their way, God will cease to be "without body, parts and passions"[2] as feminist theology takes over and worship expresses a God who is no longer "he" because he is not "it", but is gradually more "she" than "he". The "traditional sanctities" of Dom Gregory – creeds, scriptures, moral standards – will be at the mercy of ecclesiastical anarchists and iconoclasts who have already shown that they will give no quarter to those who hold to tradition. Bishops will be able to deny the basic doctrines of the faith with the only requirement their assent to the ordination of women, the one orthodoxy of the new religion – for new it is. Clergy who dissent will not be attacked physically as they were in the sixteenth century: but they may be faced with a choice between ejection or compliance.

Is that too fanciful? Hardly, for there is nothing in the last paragraph which has not been mooted in General Synod documents in the past five years. And one need only read the speeches and scribblings of the more extreme liberals – bishops, clergy and laity alike – to know that all this, together with penalties and sanctions, is part of their agenda. The chairman of the House of Laity, a professor of law no less, has said that by the Worship and Doctrine Measure, the doctrine of the Church of England is what the General Synod says is the doctrine of the Church of England. Maybe: but there would be a price to pay.

For the Synod would have succumbed to its own death wish – the seeds of which are evident enough today – and there would be no one save the remnant of the liberal élite to mourn its passing. But the Church of England is worth more than the General Synod and has survived greater crises. After all, we have God's promise that against the Church (although not necessarily the Church of England) even the gates of hell shall not prevail.

> A safe stronghold our God is still,
> A trusty shield and weapon
> He'll help us clear from all the ill
> That hath us now o'ertaken.
>
> And though they take our life,
> Goods, honour, children, wife,
> Yet is their profit small;
> These things shall vanish all.
> The city of God remaineth.[3]

George Austin is Archdeacon of York.

Notes

Apprehending joy: the imagination

1. See John Coulson *Religion and Imagination* "in aid of a grammar of assent" (Clarendon Press, 1981) pp. 82–83
2. *A Midsummer Night's Dream* V (i) 2–8, 14–22
3. The most extensive treatment of the idea of the imagination is to be found in the works of Samuel Taylor Coleridge, especially the *Biographia Literaria*, first published in 1817, a work which influenced much of the thinking about creativity in the nineteenth century (Everyman's Library, 1956). John Keats expressed the new insights with characteristic passion: "What the imagination seizes as beauty must be truth." (Letter to Benjamin Bailey, 22 November 1817)
4. Owen Barfield *The Rediscovery of Meaning and Other Essays* (Wesleyan University Press, 1977) pp. 148–149
5. The first phrase comes from David Jones's essay "Art and Sacrament" in *Epoch and Artist* (Faber, 1973) p. 167. The second phrase is from Charles Williams's essay "The Index of the Body" in *The Image of the City* ed. Anne Ridler (OUP, 1958) p. 84
6. Nicephorus (c. 758–829), Patriarch of Constantinople, writing in defence of icons. Quoted by Aidan Nicholls in *The Art of God Incarnate* (Darton, Longman and Todd, 1980) p. 85
7. "In a wholly fundamental, pragmatic sense, the poem, the statue, the sonata are not so much read, viewed or heard as they are *lived*. The encounter with the aesthetic is, together with certain modes of religious and of metaphysical experience, the most 'ingressive', transformative summons available to human experiencing. Again, the shorthand image is that of the Annunciation, of 'a terrible beauty' or gravity breaking into

the small house of our cautionary being." George Steiner *Real Presences* (Faber & Faber, 1989) p. 142

8. *Antony and Cleopatra* II (ii) 236–239
9. *Confessions* Book X, 27 translated by R. S. Pine – Coffin (Penguin, 1961)
10. "Father", "maker", "light", "came down", "ascended". All these words are inescapably metaphorical.
11. Aidan Nicholls *The Art of God Incarnate* (*supra*) p. 146

Men and women of action

1. H. F. R. Catherwood *The Christian in Industrial Society* (Tyndale Press, 1966) p. 2
2. This list is taken from a talk given by Alan Bell of PA Consulting Group on 27 September 1989 at Sundridge Park to a forum organised for *Future Perfect* by John McLean Fox, a Franciscan Tertiary.
3. John Adair *Great Leaders* (Talbot Adair Press, 1989) See *The Times* Section 3, Page I, 27 September 1989
4. Ronald Higgins *Plotting Peace. The owls reply to hawks and doves* (Brasseys, 1990) p 204. This book, to be published shortly, is the outcome of the author's work with *Dunamis*, an open forum based at St James's Church, Piccadilly.
5. Herbert Butterfield *Christianity and History* (Fontana, 1958) pp. 132–136

On Sheep and Shepherds

1. *All are Called – Towards a Theology of the Laity* (Church House Publishing, 1985)
2. "Ministry, Ministries, and the Ministry", George Carey and John Hind, in *Stepping Stones* ed. Christina Baxter, John Stott and Roger Greenacre (Hodder & Stoughton, 1987) pp. 42–67
3. Acts 21.28
4. "Clericalism, Church and Laity", Anthony Dyson in *All are Called* (*supra*) pp. 13–17

Ordination and pastoral care

1. St Ignatius *Letter to the Trallians* 2.3
2. *Baptism, Eucharist and Ministry*, Faith and Order Paper, no. 111, World Council of Churches (Geneva, 1982) p. 27
3. *Final Report* (CTS/SPCK, 1982) p. 7
4. See the *Alternative Service Book 1980*, Ordination of Priests: ordination prayer
5. *The Household of God: The Ascot Statement on Church and Ministry of the Church Union Theological Committee* (CLA, 1989) para 13, p. 6
6. *op. cit.* "Ministry and Ordination" paras 4, 5 and 7, pp. 31–33
7. *The truth shall make you free: the Lambeth Conference 1988* (Anglican Consultative Council, 1988) p. 61
8. *op. cit.* para 11, p. 5
9. *op. cit.* para 7, p. 3

Lost Sheep

1. T. S. Eliot *Four Quartets* Burnt Norton III
2. Thomas Browne *Religio Medici* (Everyman, 1956)
3. *Four Quartets* The Dry Salvages V

Education in the parish and beyond

1. See Thomas H. Groome *Christian Religious Education, Sharing our Story and Vision* (Harper & Row, 1980) chapter 9, particularly pp. 191 ff
2. John Hull *What Prevents Christian Adults from Learning?* (SCM Press, 1985) pp. 141–143
3. *Ibid* p. 141
4. *Ibid* p. 142
5. Working Party Report *All are Called* (Church House Publishing, 1985) p. 10
6. Archbishop of Canterbury's Commission Report *Faith in the City* (Church House Publishing, 1985) pp. 367–372

7. Paulo Freire *Pedagogy of the Oppressed* (Penguin Books, 1972) and *Pedagogy in Process* (Seabury Press, 1978)
8. James W. Fowler *Stages of Faith* (Harper & Row, 1981) and *Becoming Adult, Becoming Christian* (Harper & Row, 1984)
9. Thomas H. Groome *Christian Religious Education, Sharing our Story and Vision* (Harper & Row, 1980)
10. Michael Jacobs *Towards the Fullness of Christ* (Darton, Longman and Todd, 1988)
11. Anton Baumohl *Making Adult Disciples* (Scripture Union, 1984) and "Current Issues in Christian Adult Education" in the *British Journal of Theological Education* vol. 2, no. 1 (Summer, 1988)
12. Peter Ball *Journey into Faith* (SPCK, 1984) and *Adult Believing* (Mowbray, 1988)
13. Walter James "Strategies in Adult Religious Education" published in the conference papers *New Directions in Adult Religious Education No 1* (Dept of Educational Studies, University of Surrey in association with Moor Park College Trust, May 1989)
14. These ideas outlined here in brief are developed by Professor Walter James in his paper "Strategies in Adult Religious Education" (*supra*)
15. See Walter James *op. cit.*
16. These and other implications are discussed in the article by Anton Baumohl "Current Issues in Christian Adult Education" in the *British Journal of Theological Education* vol. 2, no. 1 (Summer, 1988) p. 20 ff
17. Anton Baumohl *ibid* p. 20
18. Working Party Report *Called to be Adult Disciples* (General Synod Board of Education, 1987) pp. 13, 15, 19, 23 ff
19. Walter James *op. cit.*
20. Ephesians 4. 11–12

The Church in education

1. David Newsome *Godliness and Good Learning* (John Murray, 1961)

Reflections on Synod post-Crockford

1. Dom Gregory Dix *The Shape of the Liturgy* p. 687
2. *39 Articles*: Article 1
3. Martin Luther *Ein' feste Burg*